Second Workshop of Natural Language Processing for Improving Textual Accessibility

(NLP4ITA 2013)

Atlanta, Georgia, USA
14 June 2013

Editors:

Luz Rello
Horacio Saggion
Ricardo Baeza-Yates

ISBN: 978-1-62748-991-1

Printed from e-media with permission by:

Curran Associates, Inc.
57 Morehouse Lane
Red Hook, NY 12571

Some format issues inherent in the e-media version may also appear in this print version.

Printed by Curran Associates, Inc. (2013)

Association for Computational Linguistics
209 N. Eighth Street
Stroudsburg, Pennsylvania 18360

Phone: 1-570-476-8006
Fax: 1-570-476-0860

acl@aclweb.org

Additional copies of this publication are available from:

Curran Associates, Inc.
57 Morehouse Lane
Red Hook, NY 12571 USA
Phone: 845-758-0400
Fax: 845-758-2634
Email: curran@proceedings.com
Web: www.proceedings.com

Preface

In recent years there has been an increasing interest in accessibility and usability issues. This interest is mainly due to the greater importance of the Web and the need to provide equal access and equal opportunity to people with diverse disabilities. The role of assistive technologies based on language processing has gained importance as it can be observed from the growing number of efforts (United Nations declarations on universal access to information or the WAI guidelines related to content) and research in conferences and workshops (W4A, ICCHP, ASSETS, SLPAT, etc.). However, language resources and tools to develop assistive technologies are still scarce.

This 2nd Workshop of Natural Language Processing for Improving Textual Accessibility (NLP4ITA) aimed to bring together researchers focused on tools and resources for making textual information more accessible to people with special needs including diverse ranges of hearing and sight disabilities, cognitive disabilities, elderly people, low-literacy readers and adults being alphabetized, among others.

NLP4ITA 2013 received 9 contributions from which 6 papers were accepted. We believe the accepted papers are of high quality and present a mixture of interesting topics.

We would like to thank all people who in one way or another helped in making this workshop a success. Our special thanks go to Kathleen F. McCoy for accepting to give the invited presentation, to the members of the program committee who did an excellent job in reviewing the submitted papers, to Sandra Szasz for designing and updating the NLP4ITA website, and to the NAACL organizers. Last but not least, we would like to thank our authors and the participants of the workshop.

Luz Rello, Horacio Saggion, and Ricardo Baeza-Yates
Barcelona, May 2013

Workshop Organization

Organizers:

Luz Rello, Universitat Pompeu Fabra, Spain
Horacio Saggion, Universitat Pompeu Fabra, Spain
Ricardo Baeza-Yates, Yahoo! Labs & Universitat Pompeu Fabra, Spain

Invited Speaker:

Prof. Kathleen F. McCoy, University of Delaware, USA

Program Committee:

Sandra Aluisio, Universidade de São Paulo, Brazil
Ricardo Baeza-Yates, Yahoo! Labs & Universitat Pompeu Fabra, Spain
Delphine Bernhard, University of Strassbourg, France
Giorgio Brajnik, University of Udine, Italy
Nadjet Bouayad-Agha, Universitat Pompeu Fabra, Spain
Richard Evans, University of Wolverhampton, UK
Pablo Gervás, Universidad Complutense de Madrid, Spain
Jose Manuel Gómez, Universidad de Alicante, Spain
Raquel Hervás, Universidad Complutense de Madrid, Spain
David Kauchak, Middlebury College, USA
Guy Lapalme, Université de Montreal, Canada
Elena Lloret, Universidad de Alicante, Spain
Paloma Martínez, Universidad Carlos III de Madrid, Spain
Aurelien Max, Université de Paris 11, France
Ornella Mich, Foundazione Bruno Kessler, Italy
Ruslan Mitkov, University of Wolverhampton, Spain
Paloma Moreda, Universidad de Alicante, Spain
Constantin Orasan, University of Wolverhampton, UK
Luz Rello, Universitat Pompeu Fabra, Spain
Horacio Saggion, Universitat Pompeu Fabra, Spain
Lucia Specia, University of Wolverhampton, UK
Juan Manuel Torres Moreno, University of Avignon, France
Markel Vigo, University of Manchester, UK
Leo Wanner, Universitat Pompeu Fabra, Spain
Yeliz Yesilada, Middle East Technical University, Northern Cyprus

Table of Contents

Workshop Program

Friday, June 14

9:15–9:30 Opening Remarks by Workshop Chairs

9:30–10:00 *A User Study: Technology to Increase Teachers' Linguistic Awareness to Improve Instructional Language Support for English Language Learners*
Jill Burstein, John Sabatini, Jane Shore, Brad Moulder and Jennifer Lentini

10:00–10:30 *Open Book: a tool for helping ASD users' semantic comprehension*
Eduard Barbu, Maria Teresa Martín-Valdivia and Luis Alfonso Ureña-López

10:30–11:00 Coffee Break

11:00–11:30 *Tools for non-native readers: the case for translation and simplification*
Maxine Eskenazi, Yibin Lin and Oscar Saz

11:30–12:30 Invited Talk: *Information Accessibility: More than just text deep*
Kathleen F. McCoy, University of Delaware, USA

12:30–14:00 Lunch Break

14:00–14:30 *Lexical Tightness and Text Complexity*
Michael Flor, Beata Beigman Klebanov and Kathleen M. Sheehan

14:30–15:00 *A System for the Simplification of Numerical Expressions at Different Levels of Understandability*
Susana Bautista, Raquel Hervás, Pablo Gervás, Richard Power and Sandra Williams

15:00–15:30 *A Two-Stage Approach for Generating Unbiased Estimates of Text Complexity*
Kathleen M. Sheehan, Michael Flor and Diane Napolitano

15:30–16:00 Coffee Break

16:00–17:00 Final Discussion and Closing Remarks

A User Study: Technology to Increase Teachers' Linguistic Awareness to Improve Instructional Language Support for English Language Learners

Jill Burstein, John Sabatini, Jane Shore, Brad Moulder, and Jennifer Lentini

Educational Testing Service
666 Rosedale Road, Princeton, New Jersey 08541
{jburstein, jsabatini, jshore, bmoulder, jlentini}@ets.org

Abstract

This paper discusses user study outcomes with teachers who used *Language Muse*[SM] a web-based teacher professional development (TPD) application designed to enhance teachers' linguistic awareness, and support teachers in the development of language-based instructional scaffolding (support) for their English language learners (ELL). System development was grounded in literature that supports the notion that instruction incorporating language support for ELLs can improve their accessibility to content-area classroom texts –in terms of access to content, and improvement of language skills. Measurement outcomes of user piloting with teachers in a TPD setting indicated that application use increased teachers' linguistic knowledge and awareness, and their ability to develop appropriate language-based instruction for ELLs. Instruction developed during the pilot was informed by the application's linguistic analysis feedback, provided by natural language processing capabilities in *Language Muse*.

1 Introduction

Statistics show that between 1997 and 2009 the number of ELLs enrolled in U.S. public schools has increased by 51% (National Clearinghouse for Language Acquisition, 2011). ELLs who have *lower literacy skills*, and who are reading *below* grade level may be mainstreamed into regular content-area classrooms, and may not receive supplemental English language instruction. Unfortunately, K-12 content-area teachers[1] are *less likely to be trained* to adapt their instructional approaches to accommodate the diverse cultural and linguistic backgrounds of students with varying levels of English proficiency (Adger, Snow, & Christian, 2002; Calderón, August, Slavin, Cheun, Durán, & Madden, 2005; Rivera, Moughamian, Lesaux, & Francis, 2008; Walqui & Heritage, 2012). This situation motivated the development of *Language Muse*[SM], a web-based application designed to offer teacher professional development (TPD) for content-area teachers to support their understanding of potential sources of linguistic unfamiliarity that may obscure text content for ELLs, and their ability to develop relevant language-based instructional scaffolding. We reasoned that prerequisite to effectively planning or implementing instructional supports for ELLs, teachers first needed to be able to *recognize* potential sources of linguistic difficulty. Further, teachers might need training about the specific linguistic structures that might be unfamiliar to learners, and which might lead to learners' inaccessibility to core content in text.

The motivation for *Language Muse*, thus, grew from the need to provide teachers with training about linguistic features in texts that may be unfamiliar to learners. In complement to training videos and reading resources, *Language Muse* contains a module that provides automated and explicit linguistic feedback for texts, and is intend-

[1] These are Kindergarten-12th grade teachers of subject areas, including math, science, social studies, and English language arts.

ed to support teachers in the development of lesson plans with language-based instructional activities and assessments to support reading and content comprehension of texts. The linguistic feedback module uses various natural language processing methods to provide feedback at the *vocabulary*, *phrasal*, *sentential*, and *discourse* levels. Another motivation of application was efficiency. Even with a strong linguistic awareness, manual identification of linguistic features would be a very time-consuming process.

Outcomes from pre-post teacher assessments delivered through user piloting with teachers indicated that teachers who used *Language Muse* showed gains in linguistic knowledge. Outcomes also indicated that *Language Muse* use supported teachers in the ability to develop appropriate language-based instruction for ELLs, informed by the application's linguistic analysis feedback.

2 Related Work

In a brief literature review, we address the language demands for ELLs in reading content-area texts, and the need for relevant teacher training for content-area teachers (Section 2.1). We also discuss NLP-related applications that support the linguistic analysis of texts -- typically in the context of developing *readability measures* -- which continues to be a prominent area of research; other research supports student tools allowing direct interaction with language forms (Section 2.2).

2.1 Language Demands on ELLs, and Teacher Training

Language Demands on ELLs. The English Language Arts Common Core State Standards[2] (*Standards*) (NGA Center & CCSSO, 2010) has now been adopted by 46 states and is a trend-setter in U.S. education. The *Standards* emphasize the need for all learners (including ELLs[3]) to read progressively more complex texts across multiple genres in the content areas, preparing learners for college and careers. To accomplish this, learners must have familiarity with numerous linguistic features related to vocabulary, English language structures, and a variety of text structures (discourse).

In terms of **vocabulary demands**, research reports on investigations of academic vocabulary and the *Tier* word system (Beck, McKeown, & Kucan, 2008; Calderón, 2007). Specifically, *Tier 1* words are those used in everyday conversation; *Tier 2* words are general academic words; and *Tier 3* words are found in specific domains (Beck et al, 2008; Coleman & Pimental, 2011a). All three *Tiers* are necessary to academic content learning. *Key content-area terms* in any text would include the vocabulary that students are expected to learn regardless of the *Tier*. However, there are many other vocabulary terms in the same text that may or may not be key content, but may still pose difficulties for an ELL reader. For instance, the phrase "*rock star*" is a figurative term whose meaning is not obvious from knowing the various meanings of "*rock*" or "*star*". A deficit in *morphological awareness* can be a source of reading comprehension difficulties among native speakers of English, (Berninger, Abbott, Nagy, & Carlisle, 2009; Nagy, Berninger, & Abbot, 2006), but even more so among ELLs (Carlo, August, McLaughlin, Snow, Dressler, Lippmann, & White, 2004; Kieffer & Lesaux, 2008). Teaching morphological structure has been shown to be effective with ELLs (Lesaux, Kieffer, Faller, & Kelley, 2010; Proctor, Dalton, Uccelli, Biancarosa, Snow, & Neugebauer, 2011). *Native language support* can also aid students in learning text-based content (Francis, August, Goldenberg, & Shanahan, 2004). Specifically, lessons that incorporate *cognates* (e.g., *individual* (English) and *individuo* (Spanish)) have been found to be effective in expanding English vocabulary development and aiding in comprehension (August, 2003; Proctor, Dalton, & Grisham, 2007). *Polysemous words* can contribute to overall text difficulty. Papamihiel, Lake & Rice (2005) specifically discuss difficulties of content-specific, polysemous words, where the more common meaning may lead to a misconception when using that meaning to infer the more specific content meaning (e.g., *prime* in *prime numbers*). Unfamiliar cultural references (e.g., *He's a member of the Senate.*), when reading an unfamiliar language to learn unfamiliar content, imposes a triple cognitive load for ELLs (Goldenberg, 2008).

With regard to **sentence-level demands**, long, multi-clause sentences can present frustrating

[2] http://www.corestandards.org/
[3] For details and about *Standards* and ELLs, see: http://ell.stanford.edu/.

complexities. Readers need to analyze sentence clauses to understand and encode key information in working memory as they build a coherent mental model of the meaning of a text (Kintsch, 1998). Different subject areas often have sentential and phrasal structures that are unique to that subject, resulting in comprehension breakdowns, e.g., the noun phrases in math texts "*a number which can be divided by itself* ..." (Schleppegrell, 2007; Schleppegrell & de Oliveira, 2006).

Regarding **discourse structure demands,** content-area texts may represent varying discourse relationships. Discourse relations such as, compare-contrast, cause-effect can all be intermingled within a single passage (Goldman & Rakestraw, 2000; Meyer, 2003). Teachers need to learn how to identify discourse-level information and develop scaffolding to support students' ability to navigate discourse elements in texts. Students may also be challenged in keeping track of and resolving referential (anaphoric) relationships. *Pronomial reference* can be a challenge for ELLs in texts with multiple characters or agents (Kral, 2004). An equal challenge concerns the resolution of referential relations among nouns, phrases, or ideas - a common occurrence in expository texts- whether the category of reference is pronominal, synonymy, paraphrase, or determiner, e.g., *this, that,* or *those* (Pretorius, 2005). Also critical to learning new content is understanding *connector words* functions (e.g., *because*, *therefore*) for building text cohesion (Goldman & Murray, 1992; Graesser, McNamara, & Louwerse, 2003).

Teacher Training. Teachers need to become *linguistically aware* of aspects of the English language that present potential obstacles to content access for ELLs. Yet, teachers often lack training in the identification of features of English that may challenge diverse groups of ELLs (Adger et al., 2002; Calderón et al., 2005; Rivera et al , 2008; Walqui & Heritage, 2012), and in the implementation of strategies to help ELLs academic language and vocabulary acquisition (Flinspach, Scott, Miller, Samway, & Vevea, 2008). Further, the number of teachers trained in effective instructional strategies to meet the range of needs of ELLs has not increased consistently with the rate of the ELL population (Gándara, Maxwell-Jolly, & Driscoll, 2005; Green, Foote, Walker & Shuman, 2010). Studies suggest that teachers with specialized training have a positive impact on student performance (Darling-Hammond, 2000; Peske & Haycock, 2006).

2.2 Text Accessibility and NLP

Considerable research in NLP and text accessibility has focussed on linguistic properties of text that render a text relatively more or less accessible (comprehensible). This research stream has often fed into applications offering *readability measures* – specifically, measures that predict the grade level, or grade range of a text (e.g., elementary, middle or high-school). Foundational research in this area examined the effect of morphological and syntactic text properties. Flesch (1948) reported that text features such as syllable counts of words, and sentence length were predictors of text difficulty. Newer research in this area has included increasingly more NLP-based investigations (Collins-Thompson & Callan, 2004; Schwarm & Ostendorf, 2005; Miltsakaki, 2009). Some research examines text quality in terms of discourse coherence of well-formed texts (Barzilay & Lapata, 2008; Pitler & Nenkova, 2008; Graesser, McNamara, & Kulikowich, 2011).

Human evaluation of text complexity in curriculum materials development (i.e., adaptation and scaffolding of reading texts, and the creation of activities and assessments) is a time-consuming, and typically intuitive process. Determining text complexity is also not a clear and objective measure. For example, what is complex for a native English speaker reading *on* grade level may vary from what is complex (or unfamiliar) for an ELL reading *below* grade level. This area of research continues to grow as is evidenced by NLP shared tasks (Mihalcea, Sinha & McCarthy, 2010), in the research and educational measurement communities (Burstein, Sabatini, and Shore, in press; Nelson, Perfetti, Liben & Liben, 2012).

The REAP system uses statistical language modeling to assign readability measures to Web documents (Collins-Thompson & Callan, 2004). This system is used in college-level ESL classrooms for higher level ESL students. It is designed to support automatic selection and delivery of appropriate and authentic texts to students in an instructional setting (Heilman, Zhao, Pino, & Eskenazi, 2008). Teacher users can set a number of constraints (e.g., reading level, text length, and target vocabulary) to direct the text search. The system then automatically performs the text selection. The system also has tools that allow English learners to work with the text, including dictionary definition access and vocabulary practice exercises. In pilot studies with high-intermediate learners in a university setting, a post-test showed promising learning outcomes (Heilman et al, 2008).

WERTi (Working with English Real Texts interactively) (Meurers et al., 2010) is an innovative Computer-Assisted Language Learning (CALL) tool that allows learners to interact directly with NLP outputs related to specific linguistic forms. In the context of a standard search environment, learners can select texts from the web. NLP methods are applied to identify linguistic forms that are often problematic for ELLs, including, use of determiners and prepositions, *wh*-question formation, and phrasal verbs in the texts. Meurers et al. point out that this CALL method is intended to draw learners' attention to specific properties of a language (Rutherford and Sharwood Smith , 1985). ELLs' direct interaction with different linguistic forms could support them in language skills development, and content accessibility.

To our knowledge, *Language Muse* is unique from other NLP applications in that it is designed as a teacher professional development (TPD) application intended to enhance teachers' linguistic awareness, and as a result, aid teachers in the development of language-based scaffolding to support learners' content accessibility, and language skills development. Key text complexity drivers *cannot* be communicated to teachers through numerical aggregate readability measures which appear to be the predominant approach to analysis of text difficulty described in the literature. ***Language Muse* fills a critical TPD gap.** The application is an innovative resource designed to help teachers understand the specific linguistic features that may contribute to text difficulty and ELLs' inaccessibility to text content; linguistic feedback features in SYSTEM are grounded in the literature about ELL language demands (Section 2.1).

3 *Language Muse*

Language Muse is a web-based application for enhancing teachers' linguistic awareness and supporting the development of language-based instruction for ELLs. It uses NLP methods to provide explicit linguistic feedback that is grounded in the literature discussing ELL language demands and needs (Section 2.1).

We will discuss (a) the system's specific lesson planning components, and (b) a text exploration tool that provides automated linguistic feedback.

The *lesson planning component* has three modules that support the creation of lesson plans, and related activities and assessments. To create a lesson plan, teachers complete a lesson plan template (provided by the system) with five sections commonly found in lesson plans: (a) standards and objectives, (b) formative and summative assessments, (c) engaging student interest/connecting to student background knowledge, (d) modeling and guided practice, and (e) independent practice. Teachers use system functionality to link specific texts to a lesson plan. Texts have typically been analyzed, first, using the feedback tool. Feedback is then used to *inform* lesson plan development. Activities and assessments may also be created for a specific lesson plan and will also be linked to the plan. Teachers are instructed to use linguistic feedback from the tool to develop language-focused activities and assessments that can be used to support the language objectives proposed in the lesson plan. The *Text Explorer & Adapter (TEA-Tool)* feedback module uses NLP methods for automatic summarization (Marcu, 1999); English-to-Spanish machine translation (SDL n.d.); and, linguistic feedback. A text[4], or a webpage with the relevant text is uploaded, or accessed, respectively, into the *TEA-Tool* module. The summarization capability may be used to reduce the amount of text that learners are exposed to reduce cognitive load. The machine translation capability can be used to offer native language support to learners with little English proficiency. The primary focus in this section, however, will center around the linguistic feedback that supports the *core goal* of building teachers' awareness of specific linguistic features in texts. The linguistic feedback includes specific information about vocabulary, phrasal and sentence complexity, and discourse relations. For *vocabulary*[5], categories of feedback include: academic words, cognates, collocations and figurative words and terms, cultural

[4] Microsoft Word, PDF, and Plain text files may be used.

[5] For academic words, cognates, cultural references, and homonyms, customized word lists are used. No NLP is used in these cases.

references, morphological analysis, homonyms (e.g., *their*, *there*, and *they're*), key content words, and similes[6]. For *phrasal and sentential complexity*, complex verb and noun phrases, sentences with one or more dependent clauses, and passive sentences. For *discourse*, cause-effect, compare-contrast, evidence and details, opinion, persuasion, and summary relations.

The remainder of this section describes features in the *TEA-Tool* module that use NLP to generate linguistic feedback. Providing individual evaluation descriptions for each NLP feature is beyond the scope of this paper[7], intended to focus on user study outcomes associated with *Language Muse* use (Section 4).

The specific *vocabulary* (lexical) features that use NLP methods or resources include these options[8]: *basic* and *challenge synonyms, complex and irregular word forms, variant word forms*, and *multiple word expressions*. As discussed earlier, unfamiliar vocabulary is recognized as a big contributor to text inaccessibility. The *Basic Synonym* and *Challenge Synonym* features support the vocabulary comprehension and vocabulary building aspects, respectively. To generate the greatest breadth of synonyms, the tool uses a distributional thesaurus (Lin, 1998), WordNet (Miller, 1995) and a paraphrase generation tool (Dorr and Madnani, to appear). Previous research has evaluated using these combined resources with relevant constraints to prevent too many false positives (Burstein and Pedersen, 2010). An additional slider feature allows users to adjust the number of words for which the tool will return synonyms for existing words in the text. Outputs are based on word frequency. Frequencies are determined using a standard frequency index (Breland, Jones, and Jenkins, 1994). If users want synonyms for a larger number of words across a broader frequency range that includes lower (more rare words) and higher (more common words) frequency words, then they move the slider further to the right. To retrieve synonyms for fewer and rarer words, the slider is moved to the left. For all words in the text that are within the range of word frequencies at the particular point on the slider, the tool returns synonyms. If users select *Basic Synonyms*, the tool returns all words with equivalent or higher frequencies than the word in the text. In theory, these words should be more common words that support basic comprehension. If users select *Challenge Synonyms*, then the tool returns all words with equivalent or lower frequencies than the word in the text. In this case, the teacher might want to work on vocabulary building skills to help the learner with new vocabulary. If the user selects both the *Basic Synonyms* and *Challenge Synonyms* features, then the tool will output the full list of basic (more familiar), and challenge (less familiar) synonyms for words in the text. The teacher can use these synonyms to modify the text directly, or to develop instructional activities to support word learning. The *Complex and Irregular Word Forms and Variant Word Forms* feature offers feedback related to morphological form. A morphological analyzer originally evaluated for an automated short-answer scoring system (Leacock & Chodorow, 2003) is used. This analyzer handles derivational and inflectional morphology. Feedback can be used for instructional scaffolding that includes discussion and activities related to morphological structure is an effective method to build ELLs' vocabulary. There are two features that identify words with morphological complexity, specifically, words with prefixes or suffixes: (1) *Complex and Irregular Word Forms* and (2) *Variant Word Forms*. For (1), the morphological analyzer identifies words that are morphologically complex. A rollover is available for these words. Users can place their cursor over the highlighted word, and the word stem is shown (e.g., *lost* ⇒ *stem: lose*). For (2), the system underlines words with the same stem that have different parts of speech, such as *poles* and *polar*. Teachers can build instruction related to this kind of morphological variation and teach students about variation and relationships to parts of speech.

Multiple word expressions (MWE) may include idioms (e.g., *body and soul*), phrasal verbs (e.g., *reach into*), and MWEs that are not necessarily idiomatic, but typically appear together (collocations) to express a single meaningful concept (e.g., *heart disease*). All of these MWE types may be unfamiliar terms to ELLs, and so they may interfere with content comprehension. Teachers can get feedback identifying MWEs to design relevant scaffolding for a text. To identify MWEs, two resources are used. The WordNet 3.0 compounds

[6] This new feature was not available during the pilot study.
[7] For details, see Burstein, Sabatini, Shore, Moulder, Holtzman & Pedersen (2012).
[8] These reflect the feature names in *TEA-Tool*.

list of approximately 65,000 collocational terms is used in combination with a collocation tool that was designed to identify collocations in test-taker essays (Futagi, Deane, Chodorow, & Tetreault, 2008). Some terms in the WordNet list are complementary to what is found by the collocation tool. We have found that both outputs are useful. Futagi et al.'s collocation tool identifies collocations in a text that occur in seven syntactic structures that are the most common structures for collocations in English based on The BBI Combinatory Dictionary of English (Benson, Benson, & Ilson, 1997). For instance, these include Noun of Noun (e.g., swarm of bees), and Adjective + Noun (e.g., strong tea), and Noun + Noun (e.g., house arrest). See Futagi et al. (2008) for further details.

Complex phrasal or sentential features can introduce potential difficulty in a text. A rule-based NLP module is used to identify all of these features using a shallow parser that had been previously evaluated for prepositional phrase and noun phrase detection (Leacock & Chodorow, 2003). The module to identify passive sentence construction had been previously evaluated for commercial use (Burstein, Chodorow, & Leacock, 2004). The following feedback features can be selected: *Long Prepositional Phrases*, which identifies sequences of two or more consecutive prepositional phrases (e.g., *He moved the dishes from the table to the sink in the kitchen.*); *Complex Noun Phrases*, which shows noun compounds composed of two or more nouns (e.g., emergency management agency) and noun phrases (e.g., shark-infested waters); *Passives*, which indicate passive sentence constructions (e.g., *The book was bought by the boy.*); *1+Clauses*, which highlights sentences with at least one dependent clause (e.g., *The newspaper indicated that there are no weather advisories.*); and *Complex Verbs*, which identifies verbs with multiple verbal constituents (e.g., *would have gone, will be leaving, had not eaten*).

With regard to *discourse transition features*, discourse-relevant cue words and terms are highlighted when the following discourse transitions features are identified, including: Evidence & Details, Compare-Contrast, Summary, Opinion, Persuasion, and Cause-Effect. A discourse analyzer previously evaluated for a commercial automated scoring application is used (Burstein, Kukich, Wolff, Lu, Chodorow, Braden-Harder, & Harris, 1998). The system identifies cue words and phrases in text that are being used as specific discourse (or rhetorical) contexts. For instance, "*because*" is typically associated with a cause-effect relation. However, some words need to appear in a specific syntactic construction to function as a discourse term. For instance, the word first functions as an adjective modifier and not a discourse term in a phrase, e.g., "the first piece of cake." When first is sentence-initial, as in, "First, she sliced a piece of cake," then it is more likely to be used as a discourse marker, indicating a sequence of events.

4 TPD Pilot

We report on *Language Muse* use as it was integrated into a Stanford University TPD program for in-service[9] teachers. The site agreed to integrate the application into their coursework to support coursework instruction, and instructional goals. This section describes a pilot study and outcomes with in-service teachers enrolled in the program.

4.1 Study Design

4.1.1 Site Description

Stanford University's courses are offered entirely online to teachers as part of a professional development program that awards the California State Cross-Cultural Language and Academic Development (CLAD) certificate through its California Teachers of English Learners (CTEL) certification process. By state law, all California teachers of ELLs must obtain a CLAD/CTEL or equivalent certification.

4.1.2 Teacher Participants

Responses to a background survey administered to teachers indicated a range of teaching experience from less than a year of teaching experience to as much as 37 years of teaching experience. Teachers taught across a broad range of content areas, including Art, Computers, Health, Language Arts, Math, Music, Physical Education, Science, and Social Studies, and grade levels from Kindergarten through 12th grade.

[9] This refers to teachers who have teaching credentials, and can be employed as a classroom teachers.

4.1.3 Pilot Instructional Activities[10],

After responding to the background survey, and the two pre-tests (Section 4.1.4), teachers completed the following TPD activities before moving on to post-tests (Section 4.1.4.) First, teachers read an article written by a teacher training expert on the team. The article describes best practices for developing language-based scaffolding for ELLs. The article also offers strategy descriptions as to how to use *Language Muse* to complete the lesson plan assignment (Section 4.1.4), in particular. Teachers then viewed three instructional videos that provided instruction about how to use the tool. Videos were created by a research team member, and included additional instruction about scaffolding strategies. Finally, teachers completed two practice activities with *Language Muse* which gave them an opportunity to use the different tool modules (*TEA-Tool* and lesson planning) before developing the final lesson plan assignment.

4.1.4 Measurement Instruments[11]

Teachers completed two surveys, one pre-survey, responding to questions about their professional background and school context, and a second post-survey responding to questions related to perceptions about *Language Muse* use. To evaluate teacher knowledge gains, pre- and post-test instruments were developed by the project team, and included: (a) a multiple-choice (MC) test that evaluated teachers' knowledge of linguistic structures at the Vocabulary, Sentence, and Discourse levels, and (b) a constructed- response[12] (CR) test t measured teachers' ability to identify linguistic features in a text[13] that were likely to interfere with content comprehension, and to suggest language-based instructional scaffolding to support comprehension. The pretests were administered prior to exposure to *Language Muse* (through the instructional activities (Section 4.1.3)), and the posttest after exposure. The same test was administered at pre- and post-.[14] The CR task was scored by two human raters on a 6-point scale (0 to 5, where 5=highest quality response). Inter-rater reliabilities[15] were 0.72 for Vocabulary; 0.75 for Sentences; and 0.71 for Discourse CR items. At *post-test only*, teachers developed a lesson plan using the *lesson planning* and *TEA-Tool*[16] modules in *Language Muse*. This occurred *after* teachers had completed the instructional activities included as part of *Language Muse* integration in the Stanford program. Lesson plans were evaluated by two human raters using two distinct rubrics: a) quality of *Language Skill* objectives or b) *ELL-specific Skills* objectives, i.e., unique challenges to ELLs such as, idioms or cultural references. Inter-rater reliabilities were 0.61 and 0.71 respectively. In addition, raters reviewed the linguistic feedback features that teachers had used to explore the lesson plan text, using *TEA-Tool*. The raters then examined the lesson plan and recorded the number of features explored that ended up informing the lesson plan. Inter-rater reliabilities were 0.69.

4.2 Study Results

Pre-Posttests, MC and CR. Analyses were conducted for 107 teacher participants for pre- and post-MC; 103 pre- and post-CR[17]. Paired-samples t-test showed statistically significant (p=0.02) increase in the MC Discourse score from pre-test (M =13.71, SD =2.22) to post- (M=14.20, SD =2.35; (p=0.02) increase in CR Vocabulary pre (M=2.79, SD=0.88) to post- (M=2.99, SD=0.86); in the CR Sentences score (p=0.02) from pre- (M=1.51, SD=1.23) to post- (M=1.91, SD=1.24); in the CR Total score (p=0.00) pre- (M=5.96, SD=2.35) to post- (M=6.76, SD=2.08). There were no statistically significant increases in the MC Vocabulary, Sentences, and Total scores, nor CR Discourse.

Lesson Plans. Of the 112 teachers who completed the *Lesson Plan assignment*, a significant

[10] Instructional activities are available on the *Language Muse* homepage. Teachers save all of their work in *Language Muse* so it can be viewed by course instructors and the research team, and accessed by users.

[11] For measurement instruments details, see Burstein et al, (2012).

[12] Constructed-response tasks require extended written responses.

[13] An 300-word, 8th grade Social Studies text about U.S. colonization was used.

[14] There was a lapse of approximately 8 weeks between the pre- and the post-test.

[15] Inter-rater reliabilities in this study reflect Pearson correlations.

[16] The TEA-Tool module is used to explore the linguistic features in the text; feedback features are then used to inform lesson plan development with regard to the creation of language-based scaffolding.

[17] Analyses are reported only for participants who responded to the pre- and post-.

correlation of 0.205 was found between the *Language Skills Score* and the *number of feedback features* used to inform the lesson plan.

5 Discussion and Conclusions

This paper discusses how *Language Muse*, an NLP-driven TPD application, supported K-12 teachers in understanding linguistic features in text that may be obstacles to content understanding during reading. Through the development of teachers' linguistic awareness, our original hypothesis was that teachers would become more knowledgeable about linguistic structures, and in turn, this would support them in the practice of creating lesson plans with greater coverage of text language and language objectives that would facilitate students' text and content understanding.

Study outcomes indicated that the teacher professional development package can be successfully implemented in the context of in-service, post-secondary course work. Through a study with a TPD program at Stanford University, results of the pre-post assessments administered in the study indicated at statistically-significant levels that teachers *did* improve their linguistic knowledge about vocabulary, sentences relations, and discourse relations, and that they also demonstrated and increased ability to offer language-based scaffolding strategies as evidenced by an gains pre-post total score on the CR. In the context of lesson plan development, as a secondary post-test evaluation, teachers who productively used the linguistic feedback to inform their lesson plans designed higher-quality plans (i.e., addressed language objectives that target development of new language skills), than those who did not.

The *Language Muse* TPD package is now being evaluated with nine middle-school teachers with high populations of ELLs in California, New Jersey, and Texas. After completion of the TPD, teachers will develop lesson units using *Language Muse*, and administer the lessons in their classrooms. Pre- and post-tests will be administered to students to evaluate the effectiveness of the lesson plans vis-à-vis language-based instruction.

Acknowledgments

Research presented in this paper was supported by the Institute of Education Science, U.S. Department of Education, Award No. R305A100105. Any opinions, findings, and conclusions or recommendations are those of the authors and do not necessarily reflect the IES's views. We are grateful to Steven Holtzman and Jennifer Minsky for statistical analysis support. We would like to thank Dr. Kenji Hakuta for supporting this work through his TPD program at Stanford University.

References

Adger, C. T., Snow, C., & Christian D. (2002). *What teachers need to know about language.* Washington, DC: Center for Applied Linguistics.

August, D. (2003). *Supporting the development of English literacy in English language learners: Key issues and promising practices* (Report No. 61). Baltimore, MD: Johns Hopkins University Center for Research on the Education of Students Placed at Risk.

Barzilay, Regina and Mirella Lapata (2008). 'Modeling Local Coherence: An Entity-Based Approach.' *Computational Linguistics,* 43(1): 1-34.

Beck, I. L., McKeown, M. G., & Kucan, L. (2008). *Creating robust vocabulary: Frequently asked questions and extended examples.* New York, NY: Guilford Press.

Benson, M., Benson, E., & Ilson, R. (Eds.). (1997). *The BBI Combinatory Dictionary of English: A Guide to Word Combinations.* Amsterdam & Philadelphia: John Benjamins Publishing Company.

Berninger, V., Abbot, R., Nagy, W., & Carlisle, J. (2009). Growth in phonological, orthographic, and morphological awareness in grades 1-6. *Journal of Psycholinguistic Research, 39,* 141-163.

Breland, H. Jones, R., and Jenkins, L (1994). The college board vocabulary study. Technical Report College

Burstein, J., Sabatini, J., & Shore, J. (in press). In Ruslan Mitkov (Ed.), Developing NLP Applications for Educational Problem Spaces, Oxford Handbook of Computational Linguistics. New York: Oxford University Press.

Burstein, J., Shore, J., Sabatini, J., Moulder, B., Holtzman, S., & Pedersen, T. (2012). *The Language Muse system: Linguistically focused instructional authoring* ETS RR-12-21. Princeton, NJ: ETS.

Burstein, J., and Pedersen, T. (2010). Towards Improving Synonym Options in a Text Modification Application. *University of Minnesota Supercomputing Institute Research Report Series,* UMSI 2010/165, November 2010.

Burstein, J., Chodorow, M., and Leacock, C. (2004). Automated Essay Evaluation: The Criterion Online Service, AI Magazine, 25(3), 27-36.

Burstein, J., Kukich, K., Wolff, S., Lu, C., Chodorow,

M., Braden-Harder, L., and Harris, M. D. (1998). *Automated Scoring Using A Hybrid Feature Identification Technique*. In the Proceedings of the Annual Meeting of the Association of Computational Linguistics, August, 1998. Montreal, Canada.

Calderón, M. (2007). *Teaching reading to English language learners, grades 6-12: A framework for improving achievement in the content areas.* Thousand Oaks, CA: Corwin Press.

Calderón, M., August, D., Slavin, R., Cheung, A., Durán, D., & Madden, N. (2005). Bringing words to life in classrooms with English language learners. In A. Hiebert & M. Kamil (Eds.), *Research and development on vocabulary*. Mahwah, NJ: Lawrence Erlbaum Associates.

Carlo, M. S., August, D., McLaughlin, B., Snow, C. E., Dressler, C., Lippman, D. N., & White, C. E. (2004). Closing the gap: Addressing the vocabulary needs of English language learners in bilingual and mainstream classrooms. *Reading Research Quarterly, 39,* 188-215.

Coleman, D., & Pimentel, S. (2011a). *Publishers' criteria for the Common Core State Standards in English Language Arts and Literacy, grades 3-12.* Washington, DC: National Governors Association Center for Best Practices and Council of Chief State School Officers.

Collins-Thompson, Kevyn and Jamie Callan (2004). 'A Language Modeling Approach to Predicting Reading Difficulty.' In *Proceedings of the Human Language Technology Conference of the North American Chapter of the Association for Computational Linguistics.* Boston, MA: Association for Computational Linguistics, 193-200.

Darling-Hammond, L. (2000). Teacher quality and student achievement: A review of state policy evidence. *Education Policy Analysis Archives, 8.*

Flesch, R.. (1948). A new readability yardstick. *Journal of Applied Psychology, 32*, 221-233.

Flinspach, S. L., Scott, J. A., Samway, K. D., & Miller, T. (2008, March). *Developing cognate awareness to enhance literacy: Importante y necesario.* Paper presented at the Annual Meeting of the American Educational Research Association, New York, NY..

Francis, D., August, D. Goldenberg, C., & Shanahan, T. (2004). *Developing literacy skills in English language learners: Key issues and promising practices.* Retrieved June 11, 2007, from: www.cal.org/natl-lit-panel/reports/Executive_Summary.pdf

Futagi, Y., Deane, P., Chodorow, M., & Tetreault, J. (2008). A Computational Approach to Detecting Collocation Errors in the Writing of Non-native Speakers of English, *Computer Assisted Language Learning*, Vol. 21, pp. 353–367.

Gándara, P., Maxwell-Jolly, J., & Driscoll, A. (2005). *Listening to teachers of English language learners: A survey of California teachers' challenges, experiences, and professional development needs.* Sacramento, CA: The Regents of the University of California. Retrieved from http://www.cftl.org/documents/2005/listeningforweb.pdf.

Goldenberg, C. (2008). Teaching English language learners: What the research does—and does not—say. *American Educator, 32*, 8-21.

Goldman, S. R., & Rakestraw Jr., J. A. (2000). Structural aspects of constructing meaning from text. In M. L. Kamil, P. B. Mosenthal, P. D. Pearson, & R. Barr (Eds.), *Handbook of reading research* (Vol. III, pp. 311-335). Mahwah, NJ: Lawrence Erlbaum Associates.

Graesser, Arthur C., Danielle S. McNamara, and Jonna M. Kulikowich (2011). 'Coh-Metrix: Providing Multilevel Analyses of Text Characteristics.' *Educational Researcher,* 40(5): 223-234.

Green, C., Foote, M., Walker, C., & Shuman, C. (2010). From questions to answers: Education faculty members learn about English learners. In S. Szabo, M. B. Sampson, M. M. Foote, & F. Falk-Ross (Eds.), *Mentoring literacy professionals: Continuing the spirit of CRA/ALER after 50 years* (pp. 113-125). Commerce, TX: Texas A&M University Press.

Heilman, Michael, Lee Zhao, Juan Pinto, and Maxine Eskenazi (2008). 'Retrieval of Reading Materials for Vocabulary and Reading Practice.' In *Proceedings of the Third Workshop on Innovative Use of NLP for Building Educational Applications.* Columbus, OH: Association for Computational Linguistics, 80-88.

Kieffer, M. J. & Lesaux, N. K. (2008). The role of derivational morphology in the reading comprehension of Spanish-speaking English language learners. *Reading and Writing, 21,* 783-804.

Kintsch, W. (1998). *Comprehension: A paradigm for comprehension.* Cambridge, UK: Cambridge University Press.

Leacock, C. & Chodorow, M. (2003). C-rater: Scoring of Short-Answer Questions. *Computers and the Humanities*, Vol. 37, pp. 389–405.

Lesaux, N. K., Kieffer, M. J., Faller, S. E., & Kelley, J. G. (2010). The effectiveness and ease of implementation of an academic vocabulary intervention for linguistically diverse students in urban middle schools. *Reading Research Quarterly, 45,* 196-228.

Lin, Dekang (1998). 'Automatic Retrieval and Clustering of Similar Words.' In *"Proceedings of the 17th International Conference on Computational Linguistics and the 36th Annual Meeting of the Association for Computational Linguistics.* Montreal, Canada: 768-774.

Madnani, Nitin and Bonnie J. Dorr (in press). 'Generating Targeted Paraphrases for Improved Translation.'

ACM Transactions on Intelligent Language Muses and Technology: Special Issue on Paraphrasing.

Marcu, Daniel (1999). 'Discourse Trees Are Good Indicators of Importance in Text. In *Advances in Automatic Text Summarization,* eds. Inderjeet Mani and Mark T. Maybury. Cambridge, MA: MIT Press, 123-136.

Meurers, W. Detmar, Ramon Ziai, Luiz Amaral, Adriane Boyd, Aleksandar Dimitrov, Vanessa Metcalf, and Niels Ott (2010). 'Enhancing Authentic Web Pages for Language Learners.' In *Proceedings of the NAACL HLT 2010 Fifth International Workshop on Innovative Use of NLP for Building Educational Applications,* eds. Joel Tetreault, Jill Burstein, and Claudia Leacock. Los Angeles, CA: Association for Computational Linguistics, 10-18.

Meyer, B. J. F. (2003). Text coherence and readability. *Topics in Language Disorders, 23,* 204-221.

Mihalcea, Rada, Ravi Sinha, and Diana McCarthy (2010). 'SemEval-2010 Task 2: Cross-Lingual Lexical Substitution.' In *Proceedings of SemEval-2010: Fifth International Workshop on Semantic Evaluations.* Uppsala, Sweden: Association for Computational Linguistics, 9-14.

Miller, George A. (1990). 'An On-line Lexical Database.' *International Journal of Lexicography* 3(4): 235-312.

Miltsakaki, Eleni (2009). 'Matching Readers' Preferences and Reading Skills with Appropriate Web Texts.' In *Proceedings of the European Association for Computational Linguistics.* Athens, Greece: Association for Computational Linguistics, 49-52.

Nagy, W., Beringer, V., & Abbott, R. (2006). Contributions of morphology beyond phonology to literacy outcomes of upper elementary and middle school students. *Journal of Educational Psychology, 98,* 134-147.

National Clearinghouse for English Language Acquisition (2011). *The growing numbers of English learner students.* Washington, DC: Author. Retrieved from http://www.ncela.gwu.edu/files/uploads/9/growingLEP_0809.pdf.

National Governors Association Center for Best Practices and Council of Chief State School Officers (2010). *Common Core State Standards for English language Arts & Literacy in History/Social Studies, Science, and Technical Subjects. Appendix A: Research supporting key elements of the Standards.* Washington, DC: Author.

Nelson, Jessica, Charles Perfetti, David Liben, and Meredith Liben (2012). *Measures of Text Difficulty: Testing Their Predictive Value for Grade Levels and Student Performance.* Washington, DC: The Council of Chief State School Officers. Retrieved from http://www.ccsso.org/Documents/2012/Measures%20ofText%20Difficulty_final.2012.pdf.

Pappamihiel, N. E., Lake, V., & Rice, D. (2005). Adapting a Social Studies lesson to include English language learners. *Social Studies and the Young Learner, 17,* 4-7.

Peske, H. G., & Haycock, K. (2006). *Teaching inequality: How poor and minority students are shortchanged on teacher quality.* Washington, DC: The Education Trust. Retrieved from http://www.edtrust.org/sites/edtrust.org/files/publications/files/TQReportJune2006.pdf.

Pitler, Emily and Ani Nenkova (2008). 'Revisiting Readability: A Unified Framework for Predicting Text Quality.' In *Proceedings of the 2008 Conference on Empirical Methods in Natural Language Processing.* Honolulu, HI: Association for Computational Linguistics, 186-195.

Proctor, C. P., Dalton, D., Uccelli, P., Biancarosa, G., Mo, E., Snow, C. E., & Neugebauer, S. (2011). Improving comprehension online (ICON): Effects of deep vocabulary instruction with bilingual and monolingual fifth graders. *Reading and Writing: An Interdisciplinary Journal, 24,* 517-544.

Proctor, C. P., Dalton, B., & Grisham, D. (2007). Scaffolding English language learners and struggling readers in a multimedia hypertext environment with embedded strategy instruction and vocabulary support. *Journal of Literacy Research, 39,* 71-93.

Rivera, M. O., Moughamian, A. C., Lesaux, N. K., & Francis, D. J. (2008). *Language and reading interventions for English language learners and English language learners with disabilities.* Portsmouth, NJ: Research Corporation, Center on Instruction.

Rutherford William E. and Michael Sharwood Smith (1985). 'Consciousness-Raising and Universal Grammar.' *Applied Linguistics* 6(3): 274-282.

Schwarm, Sarah E. and Mari Ostendorf (2005). 'Reading Level Assessment Using Support Vector Machines and Statistical Language Models.' In *Proceedings of the Annual Meeting of the Association for Computational Linguistics.* Ann Arbor, MI: Association for Computational Linguistics, 523-530.

Schleppegrell, M. J. (2007). The linguistic challenges of mathematics teaching and learning: A research review. *Reading and Writing Quarterly, 23,* 139-159.

Schleppegrell, M. J., & de Oliveira, L. C. (2006). An integrated language and content approach for history teachers. *Journal of English for Academic Purposes, 5,* 254-268.

SDL. (n.d.). Automated translation. Retrieved from http://www.sdl.com/en/languagetechnology/products/automated-translation/

Walqui, A., & Heritage, M. (2012, January). *Instruction for diverse groups of ELLs.* Paper presented at the Understanding Language Conference, Stanford, CA.

Open Book: a tool for helping ASD users' semantic comprehension

Eduard Barbu
University of Jaén
Paraje de Las Lagunillas
Jaén, 23071, Spain
ebarbu@ujaen.es

Maria Teresa Martín-Valdivia
University of Jaén
Paraje de Las Lagunillas
Jaén, 23071, Spain
maite@ujaen.es

Luis Alfonso Ureña-López
University of Jaén
Paraje de Las Lagunillas
Jaén, 23071, Spain
laurena@ujaen.es

Abstract

Persons affected by Autism Spectrum Disorders (ASD) present impairments in social interaction. A significant percentile of them have inadequate reading comprehension skills. In the ongoing FIRST project we build a multilingual tool called Open Book that helps the ASD people to better understand the texts. The tool applies a series of automatic transformations to user documents to identify and remove the reading obstacles to comprehension. We focus on three semantic components: an Image component that retrieves images for the concepts in the text, an idiom detection component and a topic model component. Moreover, we present the personalization component that adapts the system output to user preferences.

1 Introduction

Autism Spectrum Disorders are widespread and affect every 6 people in 10000 according to Autism Europe site[1]. The disorder is chiefly characterized by impairments in social interaction and by repetitive and stereotyped behaviour (Attwood, 2007). People affected by ASD are not able to communicate properly because they lack an adequate theory of mind (Baron-Cohen, 2001). Therefore, they are not able to infer the other persons' mental states: beliefs, emotions or desires. This lack of empathy prevents the people with ASD to have a fulfilled social life. Their inability to understand others leads to the incapacity to communicate their wishes and desires and to social marginalization.

The FIRST project seeks to make a small step towards integration of ASD people in the information society by addressing their reading comprehension ability. It is well known that many of the ASD people have a wide range of language difficulties. Psychological studies showed that they have problems understanding less common words (Gillispie, 2008), have difficulty comprehending polysemous words (Fossett and Mirenda, 2006) and have troubles dealing with figurative language (Douglas et al., 2011). The absence of good comprehension skills impedes the ASD students to participate in curriculum activities or to properly interact with their colleagues in chats or blogs. To enhance the reading comprehension of ASD people we are developing a software tool. It is built by partners in Academia and Industry in close collaboration with teams of psychologists and clinicians. It operates in a multilingual setting and is able to process texts in English, Spanish and Bulgarian languages. Based on literature research and on a series of studies performed in the United Kingdom, Spain and Bulgaria with a variety of autistic patients ranging from children to adults the psychologists identified a series of obstacles in reading comprehensions that the tool should remove. From a linguistic point of view they can be classified in syntactic obstacles (difficulty in processing relative clauses, for example) and semantic obstacles (difficulty in understanding rare or specialized terms or in comprehension of idioms, for example). The tool applies a series of automatic transformations to user documents to identify and remove the reading obstacles to comprehension. It also assists the carers , persons that assist the ASD people in every day life tasks, to correct the results of auto-

[1] http://www.autismeurope.org/

matic processing and prepare the documents for the users. This paper will focus on three essential software components related to semantic processing: a software component that adds images to concepts in the text, a software component that identifies idiomatic expressions and a component that computes the topics of the document. Moreover, we present the personalization component that adapts the system output to user preferences. The rest of the paper has the following structure: the next section briefly presents other similar tools on the market. Section 3 presents a simple procedure for identifying the obstacles ASD people have in reading comprehensions. Section 4 shows the architecture of the semantic processing components and the personalization component. The last section draws the conclusions and comments on the future work. Before presenting the main part of the article we make a brief note: throughout the paper we will use whenever possible the term "user" instead of ASD people or patients.

2 Related Work

A number of software tools were developed to support the learning of ASD people. Probably the most known one is Mind Reading[2], a tool that teaches human emotions using a library of 412 basic human emotions illustrated by images and video. Other well known software is VAST-Autism[3], a tool that supports the understanding of linguistic units: words, phrase and sentences by combining spoken language and images. "Stories about me" is an IPad application[4] that allows early learners to compose stories about themselves. All these tools and others from the same category are complementary to Open Book. However, they are restricted to pre-stored texts and not able to accommodate new pieces of information. The main characteristics that sets aside our tool is its scalability and the fact that it is the only tool that uses NLP techniques to enhance text comprehension. Even if the carers correct the automatic processing output, part of their work is automatized.

[2]http://www.jkp.com/mindreading/index.php

[3]http://a4cwsn.com/2011/03/vast-autism-1-core/

[4]http://www.limitedcue.com/our-apps/

3 Obstacles in text comprehension

Most of the automatic operations executed by the Open Book tool are actually manually performed by the carers. They simplify the parts of the text that are difficult to understand. We compared the texts before and after the manual simplification process and registered the main operations. The main simplification operations ordered by frequency performed by carers for 25 Spanish documents belonging to different genders: rent contracts, newspaper articles, children literature, health care advices, are the following:

1. Synonymous (64 Operations). A noun or an adjective is replaced by its less complex synonym.
2. Sentence Splitting (40 Operations). A long sentence is split in shorter sentences or in a bullet list.
3. Definition (34 Operations). A difficult term is explained using Wikipedia or a dictionary.
4. Near Synonymous (33 Operations). The term is replaced by a near synonym.
5. Image (27 Operations) A concept is illustrated by an image.
6. Explanation (24 Operations). A sentence is rewritten using different words.
7. Deletion (17 Operations). Parts of the sentence are removed.
8. Coreference(17 Operations). A coreference resolution is performed.
9. Syntactic Operation (9 Operations). A transformation on the syntactic parse trees is performed.
10. Figurative Language (9 Operations). An idiom or metaphor is explained.
11. Summarization (3 Operations). The content of a sentence or paragraph is summarized.

The most frequent operations with the exception of Sentence Splitting are semantic in nature: replacing a word with a synonym, defining the difficult terms. The only obstacle that cannot be tackled automatically is Explanation. The Explanation entails interpretation of the sentence or paragraph and cannot be reduced to simpler operations.

A similar inventory has been done in English. Here the most frequent operation are Sentence Splitting, Synonyms and Definition. The operations are similar across English and Spanish but their ordering differs slightly.

4 The Semantic System

In this paper we focus on three semantic components meant to augment the reading experience of the users. The components enhance the meaning of documents assigning images to the representative and difficult concepts, detecting and explaining the idiomatic expressions or computing the topics to which the documents belong.

In addition to these components we present another component called Personalization. Strictly speaking, the personalization is not related to semantic processing per se but, nevertheless, it has an important role in the final system. Its role is to aggregate the output of all software components,including the three ones mentioned above, and adapt it according to user's needs.

All the input and output documents handled by NLP components are GATE (Cunningham et al., 2011) documents. There are three reasons why GATE documents are preferred: reusability, extensibility and flexibility. A GATE document is reusable because there are many software components developed both in academy and industry, most of them collected in repositories by University of Sheffield, that work with this format. A GATE document is extensible because new components can add their annotations without modifying previous annotations or the content of the document. Moreover, in case there is no dependence between the software components the annotations can be added in parallel. Finally, a GATE document is flexible because it allows the creation of various personalization workflows based on the specified attributes of the annotations. The GATE document format is inspired by TIPSTER architecture design[5] and contains in addition to the text or multimedia content annotations grouped in Annotation Sets and features. The GATE format requires that an annotation has the following mandatory features: an id, a type and a span. The span defines the starting and the ending offsets of the annotation in the document text.

Each developed software component adds its annotations in separate name annotation sets. The components are distributed and exposed to the outside world as SOAP web services. Throughout the rest of the paper we will use interchangeably the terms: component, software component and web service.

For each semantic component we discuss:

- The reasons for its development. In general, there are two reasons for the development of a certain software component: previous studies in the literature and studies performed by our psychologists and clinicians. In this paper we will give only motivations from previous studies because the discussion of our clinicians and psychologist studies are beyond the purpose of this paper.
- Its architecture. We present both the foreseen characteristics of the component and what was actually achieved at this stage but we focus on the latter.
- The annotations it added. We discuss all the features of the annotations added by each component.

4.1 The Image Web Service

In her landmark book, "Thinking in Pictures: My Life with Autism", Temple Grandin (1996), a scientist affected by ASD, gives an inside testimony for the importance of pictures in the life of ASD people:

"Growing up, I learned to convert abstract ideas into pictures as a way to understand them. I visualized concepts such as peace or honesty with symbolic images. I thought of peace as a dove, an Indian peace pipe, or TV or newsreel footage of the signing of a peace agreement. Honesty was represented by an image of placing one's hand on the Bible in court. A news report describing a person returning a wallet with all the money in it provided a picture of honest behavior."

[5] http://www.itl.nist.gov/iaui/894.02/related_projects/tipster/

Grandin suggests that not only the ASD people need images to understand abstract concepts but that most of their thought process is visual. Other studies document the importance of images in ASD: Kana and colleagues (2006) show that the ASD people use mental imagery even for comprehension of low imagery sentences. In an autobiographic study Grandin (2009) narrates that she uses language to retrieve pictures from the memory in a way similar to an image retrieval system.

The image component assigns images to concepts in the text and to concepts summarizing the meaning of the paragraphs or the meaning of the whole document. Currently we are able to assign images to the concepts in the text and to the topics computed for the document. Before retrieving the images from the database we need a procedure for identifying the difficult concepts. The research literature helps with this task, too. It says that our users have difficulty understanding less common words (Lopez and Leekam, 2003) and that they need word disambiguation (Fossett and Mirenda, 2006).

From an architectural point of view the Image Web Service incorporates three independent subcomponents:

- **Document Indexing**. The Document Indexing sub-component indexes the document content for fast access and stores all offsets of the indexing units. The indexed textual units are words or combinations of words (e.g., terms).

- **Difficult Concepts Detection**. The difficult concepts are words or terms (e.g. named entities) disambiguated against comprehensive resources: like Wordnet and Wikipedia. This sub-component formalizes the notion "difficult to understand" for the users. It should be based on statistical procedures for identifying rare terms as well as on heuristics for evaluating the term complexity from a phonological point of view. For the time being the sub-component searches in the document a precompiled list of terms.

- **Image Retrieval**. This sub-component retrieves the images corresponding to difficult concepts from image databases or from web searching engines like Google and Bing.

The Image Web Service operates in automated mode or in on-demand mode. In the automated mode a document received by the Image Web Service is processed according to the working flow in Figure 1. In the on-demand mode the user highlights the concepts (s)he considers difficult and the web service retrieves the corresponding image or set of images. The difference between the two modes of operations is that in the on-demand mode the difficult concept detection is performed manually.

Once the GATE document is received by the system it is tokenized, POS (Part of Speech) tagged and lemmatized (if these operations were not already performed by other component) by a layer that is not presented in Figure 1. Subsequently, the document content is indexed by Document Indexing subcomponent. For the time being the terms of the document are disambiguated against Wordnet. The Image Retrieval component retrieves the corresponding images from the image database.

The current version uses the ImageNet Database (Deng et al., 2009) as image database. The ImageNet database pairs the synsets in Princeton Wordnet with images automatically retrieved from Web and cleaned with the aid of Mechanical Turk. Because the wordnets for Spanish and Bulgarian are either small or not publicly available future versions of the Web Service will disambiguate the terms against Wikipedia articles and retrieve the image illustrating the article title. All annotations are added in "ImageAnnotationSet". An annotation contains the following features:

- *Image Disambiguation Confidence* is the confidence of the WSD (Word Sense Disambiguation) algorithm in disambiguating a concept.

- *Image URL* represents the URL address of the retrieved image

- *Image Retrieval Confidence* is the confidence of assigning an image to a disambiguated concept.

In the on-demand mode the images are also retrieved from Google and Bing Web Services and the list of retrieved images is presented to the carer and/or to the users. The carer or user selects the image and inserts it in the appropriate place in the document.

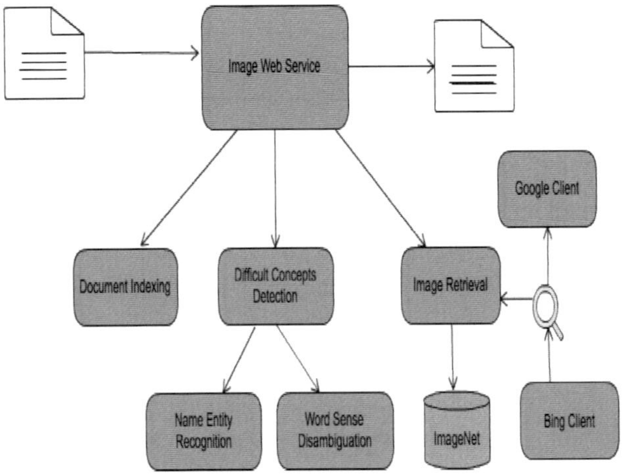

Figure 1: The Image Web Service.

4.2 The Idiom Detection Web Service

In the actual linguistic discourse and lexicographical practice the term "idiom" is applied to a fuzzy category defined by prototypical examples: "kick the bucket", "keep tabs on", etc. Because we cannot provide definitions for idioms we venture to specify three important properties that characterize them (Nunberg et al., 1994) :

- Conventionality.The meaning of idioms are not compositional.
- Inflexibility. Idioms appear in a limited range of syntactic constructions.
- Figuration. The line between idioms and other figurative language is somewhat blurred because other figurative constructions like metaphors: "take the bull by the horns" or hyperboles: "not worth the paper it's printed on" are also considered idioms.

The figurative language in general and the idioms in particular present particular problems for our users as they are not able to grasp the meaning of these expressions (Douglas et al., 2011). To facilitate the understanding of idiomatic expressions our system identifies the expressions and provide definitions for them.

The actual Idiom Web Service finds idiomatic expressions in the user submitted documents by simple text matching. The final version of Idiom Web Service will use a combination of trained models and hand written rules for idiom detection. Moreover, it is also envisaged that other types of figurative language like metaphors could be detected. At the moment the detection is based on precompiled lists of idioms and their definitions. Because the component works by simple text matching, it is language independent. Unlike the actual version of the Idiom Web Service the final version should be both language and domain dependent. The architecture of this simple component is presented in Figure 2 .

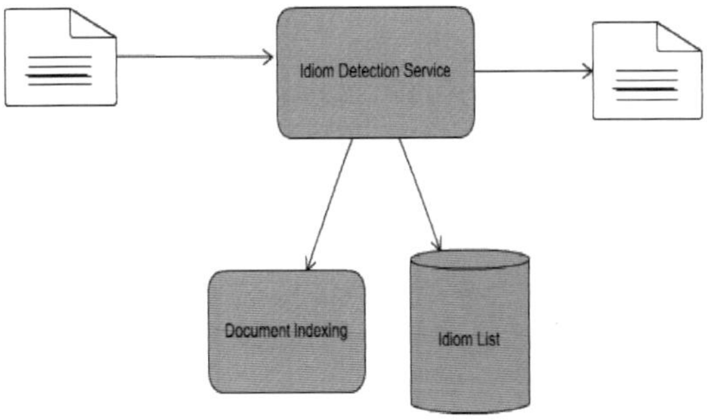

Figure 2: The Idiom Web Service.

The GATE input document is indexed by the document indexing component for providing fast access to its content. For each language we compiled list of idioms from web sources, dictionaries and Wikipedia. All idiom annotations are added in the "IdiomAnnotationSet". An annotation contains the following features:

- *Idiom Confidence* represents the confidence the algorithm assigns to a particular idiom detection.
- *Definition* represents the definition for the extracted idiom.

4.3 The Topic Models Web Service

The mathematical details of the topics models are somewhat harder to grasp but the main intuition behind is easily understood. Consider an astrobiology document. Most likely it will talk about at least three topics: biology, computer models of life and astronomy. It will contain words like: cell, molecules, life related to the biology topic; model, computer, data, number related to computer models of life topic and star, galaxy, universe, cluster related with astronomy topic. The topic models are used to organize vast collections of documents based on the themes or discourses that permeate the collection. From a practical point of view the topics can be viewed as clusters of words (those related to the three topics in the example above are good examples) that frequently co-occur in the collection. The main assumption behind Latent Dirichlet Allocation (LDA) (Blei et al., 2003), the simplest topic model technique, is that the documents in the collections were generated by a random process in which the topics are drawn from a given distribution of topics and words are drawn from the topics themselves. The task of LDA and other probabilistic topic models is to construct the topic distribution and the topics (which are basically probability distributions over words) starting with the documents in the collection.

The Topic Models Web Service is based on an implementation of LDA. It assigns topics to the user submitted documents, thus informing about the themes traversing the documents and facilitating the browsing of the document repository. The topics themselves perform a kind of summarization of documents showing, before actual reading experience, what the document is about.

The architecture of the Topic Models Web Service is presented in Figure 3.

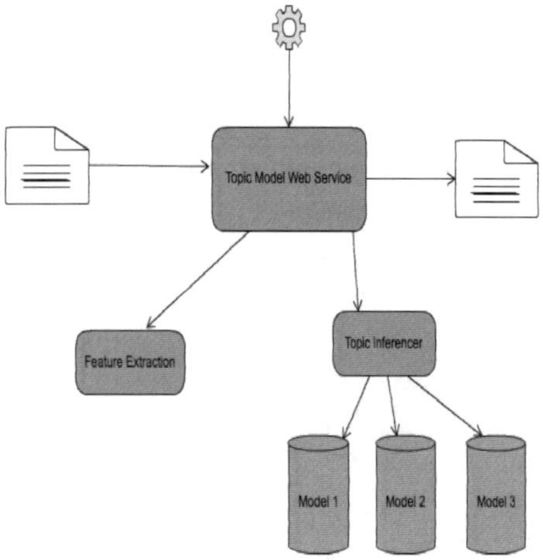

Figure 3: The Topic Model Web Service.

Once a document is received it is first dispatched to the Feature Extraction Module where it is POS tagged and lemmatized and the relevant features are extracted. As for training models, the features are all nouns, name entities and verbs in the document. Then the Topic Inferencer module loads the appropriate domain model and performs the inference and assigns the new topics to the document. There are three domains/genders that the users of our system are mainly interested in: News, Health Domain and Literature. For each of these domains we train topic models in each of the three languages of the project. Of course the system is easily extensible to other domains. Adding a new model is simply a matter of loading it in the system and modifying a configuration file.

The output of the Web System is a document in the GATE format containing the most important topics and the most significant words in the topics. The last two parameters can be configured (by default they are set to 3 and 5 respectively). Unlike the annotations for the previous components the annotation for Topic Model Web Service are not added for span of texts in the original document. This is because the topics are not necessarily words belonging to the original document. Strictly speaking the topics are attributes of the original document and therefore they are added in the "GateDocumentFeatures" section. An example of an output document containing the section corresponding to the document topics is given in Figure 4.


```
<GateDocumentFeatures>
<Feature>
  <Name className="java.lang.String">Topic-230</Name>
  <Value className="java.lang.String">contrato,concurso,empresa,acreedor,adjudicación</Valu
</Feature>
<Feature>
  <Name className="java.lang.String">Topic-12</Name>
  <Value className="java.lang.String">banco,deuda,entidad,mercado,liquidez</Value>
</Feature>
<Feature>
  <Name className="java.lang.String">Topic-61</Name>
  <Value className="java.lang.String">grupo,compañía,repsol,tener,participación</Value>
</Feature>
</GateDocumentFeatures>
```


Figure 4: The GATE Document Representation of the Computed Topic Model.

Currently we trained three topic models corresponding to the three above mentioned domains/genres for the Spanish language:

- News. The corpus of news contains more than 500.000 documents downloaded from the web pages of the main Spanish newspapers (El Mundo, El Pais, La Razon, etc...). The topic model is trained using a subset of 50.000 documents and 400 topics. The optimum number of documents and topics will be determined when the users test the component. However, one constraint on the number of documents to use for model training is the time required to perform the inference: if the stored model is too big then the inference time can exceed the time limit the users expect.

- Health Domain. The corpus contains 7168 Spanish documents about general health issues (healthy alimentation, description of the causes and treatments of common diseases, etc.) downloaded from medlineplus portal. The topic model is trained with all documents and 100 topics. In the future we will extend both the corpus and the topic model.

- Literature. The corpus contains literature in two genders: children literature (121 Spanish translation of Grimm brothers stories) and 336 Spanish novels. Since for the time being the corpus is quite small we train a topic model with 20 topics just for the system testing purposes.

For the English and the Bulgarian language we have prepared corpora for each domain but we have not trained a topic model yet. To create the training model all corpora should be POS tagged, lemmatized and the name entities recognized. The features for training the topic model are all nouns, name entities and verbs in the corpora.

4.4 Personalization

The role of the Personalization Web Service is to adapt the output of the system to the user's experience. This is achieved by building both static and dynamic user profiles. The static user profiles contain a number of parameters that can be manually set. Unlike the static profiles, the dynamic ones contain a series of parameters whose values are learnt automatically. The system registers a series of actions the users or carers perform with the text. For example, they can accept or reject the decisions performed by other software components. Based on editing operations a dynamic user profile will be built incrementally by the system. Because at this stage of the project the details of the dynamic profile are not yet fully specified we focus on the static profile in this section.

The architecture of the Personalization component is presented in Figure 5.

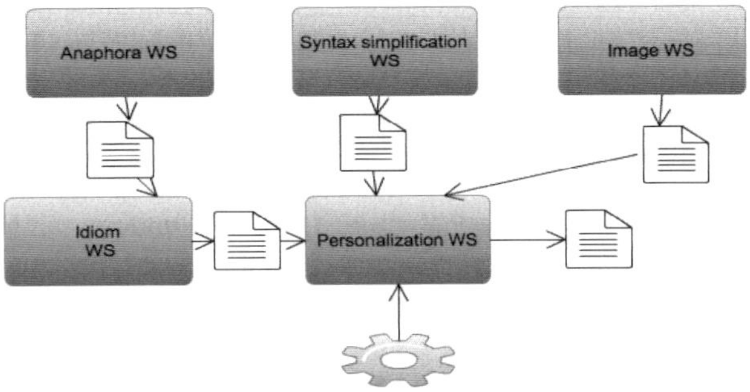

Figure 5: The Personalization Web Service.

In addition to the web services presented in the previous sections (The Idiom Web Service and The Image Web Service) the Personalization Web Service receives input from Anaphora Web Service and Syntax Simplification Web Service. The Anaphora component resolves the pronominal anaphora and the Syntax Simplification component identifies and eliminates difficult syntactic constructions. The Personalization component aggregates the input from all web services and based on the parameters specified in the static profile (the wheel in Figure 5) transforms the aggregate document according to the user preferences. The personalization parameters in the static profile are the following:

1. *Image Disambiguation Confidence.* The image annotation is dropped when the corresponding concept disambiguation confidence is less than the threshold.

2. *Image Retrieval Confidence.* The image annotation is dropped when the assigned image is retrieved with a confidence lower than the threshold.

3. *Idiom Confidence.* The idiom annotation is dropped when the assigned idiom confidence is less than the threshold.

4. *Anaphora Confidence.* The pronominal anaphora annotations are dropped when the anaphor is solved with a confidence less than the threshold.

5. *Anaphora Complexity.* The parameter assess the complexity of anaphors. If the anaphora

complexity score is less than the specified threshold it drops the resolved pronominal anaphora.

6. *Syntactic Complexity.* It drops all annotations for which the syntactic complexity is less than the threshold.

The user can also reject the entire output of a certain web service if he does not need the functionality. For example, the user can require to display or not the images, to resolve or not the anaphora, to simplify the sentences or not, etc. In case the output of a certain web service is desired the user can specify the minimum level of confidence accepted. Any annotation that has a level of confidence lower than the specified threshold will be dropped. In addition to the parameters related to document content the static profile includes parameters related to graphical appearance (e.g. fonts or user themes) that are not discussed here.

5 Conclusions and further work

In this paper we presented three semantic components to aid ASD people to understand the texts. The Image Component finds, disambiguates and assigns Images to difficult terms in the text or related to the text. It works in two modes: automated or on-demand. In the automated mode a document is automatically enriched with images. In the on-demand mode the user highlights the concepts (s)he considers difficult and the web service retrieves the corresponding images. Further development of this component will involve disambiguation against Wikipedia and retrieval of images from the corresponding articles. The Idiom Component finds idioms and other figurative language expressions in the user documents and provides definitions for them. Further versions of the component will go beyond simple matching and will identify other categories of figurative language. The Topic Models component helps organizing the repository collection by computing topics for the user documents. Moreover it also offers a summarization of the document before the actual reading experience. Finally the Personalization component adapts the system output to the user experience. Future versions of the component will define dynamic user profiles in addition to the static user profiles in the current version. Our hope is that the Open Book tool will be useful for other parts of populations that have difficulties with syntactic constructions or semantic processing, too.

Acknowledgments

We want to thank the three anonymous reviewers whose suggestions helped improve the clarity of this paper. This work is partially funded by the European Commission under the Seventh (FP7 - 2007-2013) Framework Program for Research and Technological Development through the FIRST project (FP7-287607). This publication reflects only the views of the authors, and the Commission cannot be held responsible for any use which may be made of the information contained therein.

References

Tony Attwood. 2007. *The complete guide to Asperger Syndrome*. Jessica Kingsley Press.

Simon Baron-Cohen. 2001. Theory of mind and autism: a review. *Int Rev Ment Retard*, 23:169–184.

David M. Blei, Andrew Y. Ng, and Michael I. Jordan. 2003. Latent dirichlet allocation. *J. Mach. Learn. Res.*, 3:993–1022, March.

Hamish Cunningham, Diana Maynard, Kalina Bontcheva, Valentin Tablan, Niraj Aswani, Ian Roberts, Genevieve Gorrell, Adam Funk, Angus Roberts, Danica Damljanovic, Thomas Heitz, Mark A. Greenwood, Horacio Saggion, Johann Petrak, Yaoyong Li, and Wim Peters. 2011. *Text Processing with GATE (Version 6).*

Jia Deng, Wei Dong, R. Socher, Li-Jia Li, Kai Li, and Li Fei-Fei. 2009. ImageNet: A large-scale hierarchical image database. In *Computer Vision and Pattern Recognition, 2009. CVPR 2009. IEEE Conference on*, pages 248–255. IEEE, June.

K.H. Douglas, K.M. Ayres, J. Langone, and V.B. Bramlett. 2011. The effectiveness of electronic text and pictorial graphic organizers to improve comprehension related to functional skills. *Journal of Special Education Technology*, 26(1):43–57.

Brenda Fossett and Pat Mirenda. 2006. Sight word reading in children with developmental disabilities: A comparison of paired associate and picture-to-text matching instruction. *Research in Developmental Disabilities*, 27(4):411–429.

William Matthew Gillispie. 2008. *Semantic Processing in Children with Reading Comprehension Deficits*. Ph.D. thesis, University of Kansas.

Temple Grandin. 1996. *Thinking In Pictures: and Other Reports from My Life with Autism*. Vintage, October.

Temple Grandin. 2009. How does visual thinking work in the mind of a person with autism? a personal account. *Philosophical Transactions of the Royal Society B: Biological Sciences*, 364(1522):1437–1442, May.

Rajesh K. Kana, Timothy A. Keller, Vladimir L. Cherkassky, Nancy J. Minshew, and Marcel Adam Just. 2006. Sentence comprehension in autism: Thinking in pictures with decreased functional connectivity.

B. Lopez and S. R. Leekam. 2003. Do children with autism fail to process information in context ? *Journal of child psychology and psychiatry.*, 44(2):285–300, February.

Geoffrey Nunberg, Ivan Sag, and Thomas Wasow. 1994. Idioms. *Language*.

Tools for non-native readers: the case for translation and simplification

Maxine Eskenazi
Language Technologies Institute
Carnegie Mellon University
Pittsburgh PA 15213
max@cmu.edu

Yibin Lin
Language Technologies Institute
Carnegie Mellon University
Pittsburgh PA 15213
yibinl@cs.cmu.edu

Oscar Saz
Language Technologies Institute
Carnegie Mellon University
Pittsburgh PA 15213
osaz@cs.cmu.edu

Abstract

One of the populations that often needs some form of help to read everyday documents is non-native speakers. This paper discusses aid at the word and word string levels and focuses on the possibility of using translation and simplification. Seen from the perspective of the non-native as an ever-learning reader, we show how translation may be of more harm than help in understanding and retaining the meaning of a word while simplification holds promise. We conclude that if reading everyday documents can be considered as a learning activity as well as a practical necessity, then our study reinforces the arguments that defend the use of simplification to make documents that non-natives need to read more accessible.

1 Introduction

There are many tools that natural language processing (NLP) can offer disadvantaged readers to aid them in understanding a document. Readers may be at a disadvantage due to poor sight, to cognitive disabilities, or simply to reading in a language other than their native one (L1). This paper addresses that last case. For non-native readers, there are a number of aids that could be made available to them. Some aids help on the word level, assuming that the understanding of a specific word is what is impeding comprehension. Others address a more global level, presuming that the understanding blockage is due lack of comprehension of the meaning of a group of words. Our work addresses learning English vocabulary, for which we have conducted studies on both word-level and higher-level aids. We argue that our findings can inform what can be done to make documents more understandable in general for non-natives.

In the past, we have studied the effect of aids such as ordered definitions (Dela Rosa and Eskenazi, 2011) and synthesized speech (Dela Rosa et al., 2010) on learning vocabulary from web documents. These aids have been aimed at the word level and have been shown to help learning. We explored the wider context around an unknown word in an effort to give the non-native reader an understanding of the several-word context around an unknown word in order to help understanding of the meaning of the text.

Reading documents to learn a language is a very different activity from reading an everyday document (like a rental agreement) out of necessity. Yet we find that there are similarities between the two activities. We believe that, unlike for some other categories of disadvantaged readers, each document that a non-native reads is a learning moment and that they learn the target language more with each encounter. These incremental additions to the readers' knowledge enable them to be increasingly capable of tackling future unknown documents. It also reflects on the manner with which readers tackle a document since some understanding of the words has to take place in order for the document to be understood. We believe that these similarities warrant using learning findings to guide the choice of NLP tools used in document processing for non-native readers. The learning environment is used in this paper to measure document understanding.

2 Background

Using learning as a means of estimating the usefulness of NLP techniques in making texts more accessible, we can examine the positions that the learning community has taken on the educational value of several of these techniques.

Translation (the use of L1 in second language (L2) vocabulary acquisition) is the area in which we find the greatest controversy. Models of L2 lexical acquisition represent acquisition of new L2 words as an assimilation through an L1 lemma that is generalized and applied to concepts in L2 (Jiang, 2000; Kroll and Sunderman, 2003). Excessive use of L1 is believed to reduce L2 fluency and to fossilize errors. Context, dictionary definitions and examples of other sentences in which a word could be used are commonly considered to be the most effective tools since students can interiorize the concept of the new word without reliance on L1. This implies that the use of such techniques can lead to better learning and improved fluency than direct use of L1 translation. This claim has been challenged by Grace (1998), showing that that when translation is provided, there are higher scores on vocabulary tests both in the short-term and long-term use of the new words. Prince (1996) also claimed that the more proficient students benefit more from translation on short-term lexical recall tasks, since it is easier for them to get rid of the L1 scaffolding. These studies and others have been hampered by the ability to accurately measure the extent of the subjects' use of translation. The REAP software described below has afforded a more precise estimate of use and of retention of vocabulary items.

Simplification has had more widespread acceptance. Simplified texts have often been provided to language learners either along with the original text or alone (Burstein et al, 2007, Petersen and Ostendorf, 2007). These texts have been used as reading comprehension exercises or textbook reading materials (Crossley, et al. 2007). According to Oh (2008), simplification typically uses shorter sentences, simpler grammar and controlled vocabulary. The use of simplified texts has been shown to significantly help students' reading comprehension (Yano, et al. 1994, Oh 2008). However, there has not been any research specifically about whether reading the simplified texts, rather than the original ones, will affect the students' vocabulary acquisition. There are a few disadvantages related to simplifying texts for ESL students. Yano et al. (1994) note that simplified texts may appear unnatural, giving them a lack of flow, thus making them difficult to read. They may also lack the complex grammar structures that commonly exist in the real world (that students should be exposed to). The simplified texts used in these studies were created by hand and are usually written with the express intention of featuring certain vocabulary and/or syntactic elements for the purpose of being used by a non-native learner.

To address the link between vocabulary and comprehension of a text, the literature often reveals mastery of vocabulary as the key. Perfetti (2010) emphasized the vocabulary-comprehension link. Increased vocabulary has been shown to increase comprehension. Thus text comprehension for non-natives could depend on either presenting only words that they can understand or offering an aid for understanding any challenging words that they may encounter.

2.1 NLP techniques

Assuming that we can aid a non-native in understanding a document by using natural language processing techniques, numerous possibilities present themselves. We can help the student both on the word level and on a more global (contextual) level. On the word level, the one aid that does not appear to need any processing is dictionary definitions. Access to an online dictionary would give the student definitions to any word in question. However, many words are polysemous, often having several meanings for the same part of speech (like "bank"). In that case, the reader has to choose which one of the meanings is the right one for the context of the text at hand. This dilemma (and possible incorrect choice) can be avoided by using word sense disambiguation (Dela Rosa and Eskenazi 2011). We showed that when definitions are presented in an ordered list, according to the best fit in the context, students learned words better. Another word-level aid is the use of speech synthesis to speak the word to the reader (Dela Rosa 2010). Non-natives know some words aurally, but have never seen them in written form. This aid is especially helpful when the orthography of an unknown word makes it difficult to deduce the pronunciation (as in "thought"). Another aid presents a word in other contexts. Giving the student the ability to compare several contexts with their contrasting meanings is helpful for learning. These contexts can be found by searching for sentences with a target word and a set of commonly co-occurring context words.

While research in vocabulary acquisition over the years has shown positive results for many word-centric learning aids, it is interesting to expand the offerings to context-level aids. We were also curious to see if the use of the REAP platform (Brown and Eskenazi, 2005) could help add to the knowledge of the role of translation in L2 vocabulary learning. This is what brought us to examine the effect of translation and simplification on learning. These two techniques, thanks to the use of NLP, could be totally automated in the future. Research in machine translation (MT) goes back several decades and many types of statistical models have been employed (Koehn, 2010). If all of the documents to be translated are in one given domain, then sufficiently good automatically translations can be obtained.

Automated simplification is a newer domain. There has been significant progress in simplifying documents for use by specific disadvantaged populations (Alusio et al 2010, Bach et al, 2011, Chandrasekar and Srinivas, 1997, Inui et al, 2003, Medero and Ostendorf, 2011, Yaskar et al 2010). Like Alusio and colleagues, who work with low-literacy populations, and a few other authors, we are concerned not only about the quality of the simplification, but also about whether the simplified documents actually help disadvantaged readers.

We could have also looked at summarization, which uses some of the same techniques that are used for simplification. In some early unpublished studies, we found that students experienced difficulty when asked to summarize a passage. They usually responded by simply cutting and pasting the first sentence of that passage. This could have meant that students just could not produce a well-structured sentence and thus avoided doing so. But non-natives, who are asked to identify the appropriate summary out of four possibilities in a multiple choice question, *also* had much difficulty. Thus, rather than giving a very high-level overview of a passage through summarization, we chose to look at the intermediate level aids that would also contribute to vocabulary understanding: translation and simplification of local contexts.

Translation and simplification can both be characterized as relating to overall context, operating effectively on a string of several words rather than on only one word. They both aid in understanding the meaning of the whole string as opposed to just one target word, and their help for unknown words is through making the context of the word clear enough to surmise the meaning of the word. Besides its controversial status, translation had also attracted our interest when we observed the students' efforts to get translations for tasks in class. We wanted to find out if translation had different properties from all other aids. Translation is different from the aids that we had used in the past in two ways:

- it uses L1
- it covers several-word contexts, rather than just one word.

To tease apart these two characteristics, we became interested in simplification, which shares the second characteristic, but not the first.

3 The REAP tutor

The studies in this paper used the CMU REAP intelligent tutor. That tutor provides curriculum for vocabulary acquisition for non-native students while serving as a platform for research studies (Brown and Eskenazi, 2005). REAP gives students texts retrieved from the Internet that are matched to their reading level and their preferences (Heilman et al., 2008) and helps them acquire new words from context (Juffs et al., 2006). REAP incorporates several features like pop-up word definitions, examples of the word in other contexts, text-to-speech synthesis of words and translation of words to the student's native language.

REAP presents the reading in any web browser (see Figure 1). Upon registration, students enter their native language. To get a definition, clicking on a word brings up a pop-up window showing the definition and examples of use of that word and a button for hearing the pronunciation of the word. Focus words, the words that the teacher has chosen for the students to learn, are highlighted in the text.

From the beginning, REAP has shown that it can improve students' acquisition of new vocabulary in English (Heilman et al., 2006). Features embedded in REAP have been validated in several experimental studies which showed the learning outcomes achieved by the students. REAP has been used to study motivation as well as learning gains.

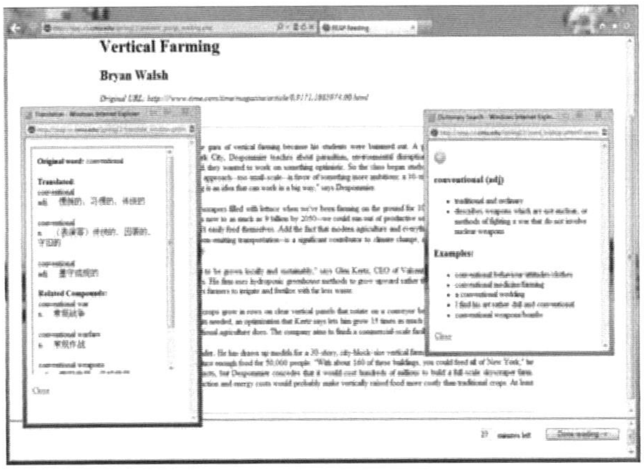

Figure 1. REAP interface and features for a student whose native language is Mandarin.

4 The translation study

REAP was used to study whether translation helped students to learn vocabulary (Lin, Saz and Eskenazi, in review). These studies explored whether the students both learned more and became more fluent when they use translation. It is challenging to measure fluency. While it is impossible to record everything that the student says in her everyday conversations and then measure the average rapidity of response, one can measure the increase in the rapidity of response from the moment an item (post-test question) appears on the screen to when the student clicks on the answer and can compare results for that student as well as across groups of students. The documents used in this study were gathered from a crawl of the internet for documents containing certain focus words that students were to learn. The documents were filtered to be at the level of the students and the topics were varied, from sports to current events, for example. The translation (bilingual dictionary) of the words in this study was provided by WordReference.com and the Bing Translator (http://www.microsofttranslator.com/) for the documents (contexts) in the study. The translations of all of the focus words in all of the students' L1s were manually checked by native speakers to make sure that the translated word corresponded with the specific context in which it appeared. If necessary, a change in the translation was made to make it context-appropriate.

All studies described in this paper were included as regular curricula at the English Language Institute of the University of Pittsburgh. The first study involved 27 students taking the Level 5 Reading course (high-intermediate learners); 25 were native speakers of Arabic, 1 spoke Spanish and 1 spoke Turkish. The second study involved 26 students in Level 5: 22 of them were native Arabic speakers, 2 were Mandarin Chinese speakers and 2 were Korean speakers. There were two studies to determine whether the way that the students requested translations had an effect on the amount of translations they asked for.

For both studies, the first session consisted of a pre-test which measured knowledge of a set of focus words in multiple-choice cloze questions (Taylor 1953), where the target word was removed from a full, meaningful sentence. There were 2 questions per focus word. Post-reading (immediately after reading a document) and post-test (after all the training sessions were over) questions had the same form as the pre-test and involved completely different sentences.

In each training session, students had one 400-500 word reading. After each reading, they took the post-reading test where they answered 2 previously unseen cloze questions per focus word. The students were shown their results along with the correct answers to the cloze questions at the end of each post reading test. In the last session, the students took a post-test with content similar to the pre-test, 2 new unseen questions per focus word.

The first study took place for 8 weeks in the fall of 2011. Each reading session had one reading prepared for the students with 4 focus words, for a total of 24 focus words. The second study took place for 6 weeks in the spring of 2012. There were also 24 focus words in this study.

The main difference in the setup of both studies was how the students accessed a translation. For the fall 2011 study students had to type or copy and paste one or more words into a box at the bottom of the screen to get the translation. In the spring 2012 study they used a left mouseclick to get the translation. In both studies, the students could click (left mouseclick in fall 2011 and right mouseclick in spring 2012) to obtain the definition from the Cambridge Advanced Learners' Dictionary (CALD, Walter, 2005) and to listen to text-to-speech synthesis of the word (Cepstral, 2012).

The accuracy of each student at the pre-test, post-reading and post-test was calculated as the percentage of correct answers over the total number of questions in the test. The fluency was calculated as the median response time of a given student to answer each question. To measure fluency, we used the median and not the mean of the response times since the mean was distorted by a few instances of very long response duration for a few questions (possibly due to distractions). We also used comparative measures, such as gain and normalized gain in accuracy between two different assessment tasks (for instance, from pre-test to post-test) (Hake, 1998). A positive value of the gain and the normalized gain means that the student achieved higher scores in the post-test.

We note that only 14 (17%) of the translations are for focus words.

The results show that students used translation when it was easier (clicking instead of typing), in detriment to using dictionary definitions. Students did not request definitions or translations for all of the focus words. This may indicate that they are not indiscriminately clicking on words, as has sometimes been seen in the past. Rather they may be making an effort to click on words they felt they did not know well.

	Dictionary		Translation	
	All words	Focus words	All words	Focus words
Fall'11	5.29	2.35	2.31	0.64
Spring'12	1.78	0.84	8.15	2.35

Table 1. Use of dictionary and translation (4 focus words/reading in Fall'11, 3 focus words/reading in Spring'12). Average is per student and per reading.

We then examined the accuracy of the students for just the words that they chose to translate. Table 2 shows that accuracy increases in post-reading tests and post-tests with respect to the pre-test for both studies. But there is a drop in the post-test scores with respect to the post-reading tests in spring 2012. Furthermore, there is an increase in response time in the post-test, which is more pronounced for spring 2012. These are the first indications of possible differences in student performance related to their patterns in the use of translations.

	Accuracy			Fluency	
	Scores (mean and standard deviation)			Response time (median value)	
	Pre-test	Post-reading	Post-test	Pre-test	Post-test
Fall '11	0.35±0.15	0.67±0.11	0.65±0.08	20 sec.	22 sec.
Spring' 12	0.48±0.25	0.74±0.16	0.62±0.17	18 sec.	23.5 sec.

Table 2. Accuracy and fluency results for *translated* words.

To find whether the amount of translation actually affected this result, spring 2012 students were separated into 2 groups: the 13 students who used the least number of translations overall and the 13 students who used the most translations. Figure 2 shows the normalized gains in post-reading tests and post-tests over the pre-test for these 2 groups. Both groups present a similar gain in post-reading (approximately 0.35) and, while this gain was lower for groups on the post-test, the students who used translation the most had a larger loss. Although not significant ($p = 0.48$), this difference, which is approximately 0.07 in normalized gain, indicates that these students are having more difficulty transferring the knowledge they may have acquired in the longer term. The low significance is mainly due to the relatively small number of participants in the study.

5 The simplification study

In this study the setup, using REAP as the platform, was similar to the translation study. The students could click right for translations or left for simplifications and could type a word in a box at the bottom of the screen for definitions. Translations and simplifications could be for one or several words at a time. The number of questions on focus words (24 words this time), over the pretest, post-reading test and the post-test remained the same. There were 20 students in this study. There were 11 speakers of Arabic, 3 of Japanese, 2 each of Korean and Chinese and one each of Spanish and Serbo-Croatian.

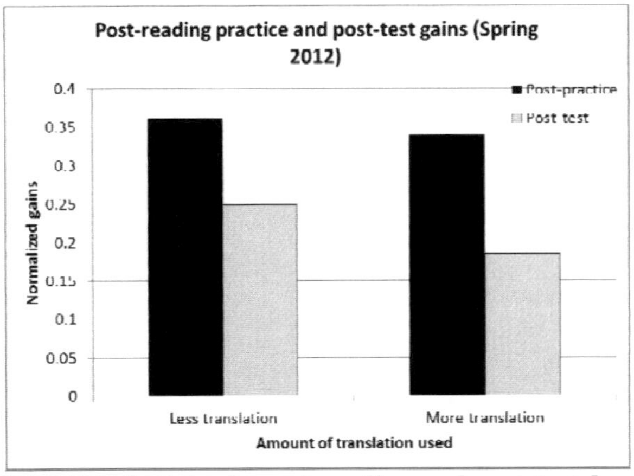

FIGURE 2. Gains in post-reading and post-test depending on the amount of translation used

Again, the translations were carried out automatically as described above, with a human verification pass. The simplifications were created by one of the authors by replacing less frequent words with appropriate more frequent ones (Leroy and Endicott, 2011) and splitting complex sentences into shorter ones. An example of a simplification:

> <u>for</u>: " They began immigrating in large numbers in the 1960s for economic reasons and now make up a third of the population—but there are also Africans, West Indians, Pakistanis, Indians, Turks, Chinese, and Eastern Europeans."
>
> <u>the simplified form was</u>: "They began immigrating in large numbers in the 1960s for economic reasons. These people now make up a third of the population. There are also Africans, West Indians, Pakistanis, Indians, Turks, Chinese, and Eastern Europeans."

Overall, they requested 218 simplifications, 82 translations and 79 dictionary lookups. This was surprising to us. Given the large number of translation requests in the past two studies, we were prepared to see overwhelmingly more clicks for translations than for simplifications. This result is important in deciding what aids can be given to non-native readers. While we thought that a reader would prefer an aid that involved translation, this result shows an acceptance of the L2 aid. Non-natives probably realize the educational value of the L2 tool and voluntarily choose to use it.

Only 14 (17%) of the translations contained focus words while 102 (47%) of the simplifications did. Given the small number of focus word translations, results cannot be significant. REAP significantly helps students to learn focus words in general ($p<0.05$). Post-reading tests show lower accuracy than the post-test. The t-test shows that the difference here is not statistically significant ($p=0.26$).

To control for the quality of the study, we compared overall learning gains from this study with that of the two translation studies above on Table 3 and found them to be similar

	Normalized Gain	
	Pre-test to Post-reading	Pre-test to post-test
Fall'12	**0.10 ± 0.24**	**0.17 ± 0.28**
Fall'11	0.31 ± 0.33	0.31 ± 0.28
Spring'12	0.35 ± 0.28	0.22 ± 0.21

Table 3. Learning Outcome: Gains (gain + deviation)

Figure 3 shows the number of requests for simplification and translation for each of the six documents in the study compared to their readability level (Heilman 2008). We note that the hardest document (#6) was not the one for which the most aid was requested. This could simply be due to the decreasing number of requests for aid over time.

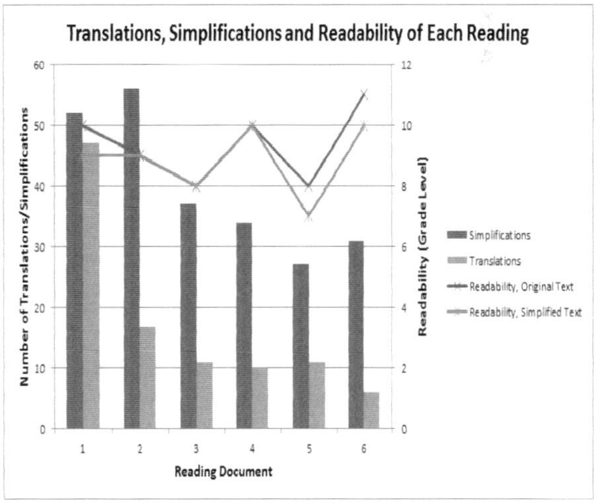

Figure 3: Readability vs number of translations and simplifications

To control for any outlier document, we also looked at whether any one of the six documents required more translation than simplification. Figure 3 also shows that the trend to request more simplification held true for all of the documents. We note that this can only be called a trend due to the significant standard deviation which, in turn, is due to the low number of participants. The first document was where the requests for the two were almost equal. This could be due to the students trying out both possibilities to see what they liked or to the fact that over a short time they realized the greater value of the L2 aid.

Table 4 shows the normalized gains for focus words that were translated or simplified. The low number of translation requests lead to results that are not significant. We note that for simplification there is a trend implying learning gains at both the post-reading test and, in long term retention, for the post-test.

Normalized gain			
Aid	pre-test to post-reading	pre-test to post-test	No. items
Translation	-0.07 ± 0.15	0.22 ± 0.13	14
Simplification	0.27 ± 0.17	0.28 ± 0.18	98

Table 4: Normalized Gain (average and standard deviation) for focus words that were translated or simplified and number of clicks on focus words

Normalized Gain			
	Pre-test to post-reading	Pre-test to post-test	no. of questions
Focus words not translated	0.06±0.26	0.17±0.30	946
Focus words not simplified	0.06±0.26	0.18±0.31	862

Table 5: Normalized Gain (average and standard deviation) for focus words that were *not* translated or simplified and number of questions

In the case of non-translated and non-simplified focus words, although there was also some room for improvement (and at first, it would seem that the learning gains are larger), there are some variables that have not been taken into account here. One is that a subject could have often requested *definitions*. Some subjects may benefit more from the use of the definitions than from other types of help. We will test this hypothesis in the future, when we have more data, to see if the benefits from each type of help are greater for some subjects than for others. While we are not convinced that this is the cause for the differences we see here, we do believe that *hearing the words* when working through the documents may be a factor. Since the students only have the written form of the word at pre-test time, they may know the word to hear it, but not by sight. In past years in our use of REAP in the classroom, we have noticed many students suddenly recognizing a word after hearing it (from clicking on the synthesis option). Again due to lack of sufficient data, we cannot explore this further for this dataset, but plan to look at this and any other possible variables in the near future.

6 Conclusions and further directions

We have argued that exploring the learning results of non-natives when using various aids for learning vocabulary through context may guide our choices of reading aids for this population.

We have specifically explored the use of translation and of simplification. Both simplification and translation are voluntarily used by students and when both are available, students tend to prefer simplification. This should make the use of simplified documents in real life reading situations very acceptable to non-natives.

The overuse of translation contributes to a decline in long term retention of new vocabulary while the use of simplification appears to aid in retention. This could mean that reading any simplified document may benefit the ever-learning non-native when encountering future documents.

In REAP, we collect documents from the Internet and characterize them by reading level. We also characterize them by topic (sports, health, etc). While we choose these documents to keep up the students' interest, they in no way represent the real challenges of dealing with a rental agreement, a bank loan document, etc. While REAP does instill fundamentals of vocabulary understanding, it does not have the student apply this knowledge to the situations that are encountered in the real world. This is an essential need that can be fulfilled by members of the NLP community working together to create a database of real life challenging documents that can be annotated and used as a basis of comparison of research results. These documents should also be annotated for readability, etc. Such a realistic database can then serve the community as a whole as it develops novel and robust simplification tools.

ACKNOWLEDGEMENTS

This work is supported through the Refinement and Fluency Thrust of the Pittsburgh Science of Learning Center which is funded by the US National Science Foundation under grant number SBE-0836012. Any opinions, findings, and conclusions or recommendations expressed in this material are those of the authors and do not necessarily reflect the views of the NSF. Oscar Saz was supported with a Fulbright/MEX fellowship.

References

Alusio, S., Specia, L., Gasperin, C., Scarton, C., 2010, Readability Assessment for Text Simplification, Proc NAACL HLT Fifth Workshop on Innovative Use of NLP for Building Educational Applications, p. 1-9.

Bach, N., Gao, Q.,Vogel, S., Waibel A., 2011, TriS: A Statistical Sentence Simplifier with Log-linear Models and Margin-based Discriminative Training In Proceedings of the 5th International Joint Conference on Natural Language Processing (IJCNLP 2011), Chiang Mai, Thailand.

Brown, J., Eskenazi, M., 2005, Student, text and curriculum modeling for reader-specific document retrieval, In Hamza, M.-H. (Ed.) Proceedings of the IASTED International Conference on Human-Computer Interaction (pp. 44-47). Anaheim, CA: Acta Press.

Burstein, J., Shore, J., Sabatini, J., Lee, Y., Ventura, M., 2007, The automated text adaptation tool, in Demo proceedings of NAACL-HLT, Rochester.

Cepstral Text-to-Speech, 2000, Retrieved Sep. 8, 2012, from http://www.cepstral.com/.

Chandrasekar, R. and Srinivas, B., 1997, Automatic induction of rules for text simplification. Knowledge-Based Systems, 10(3):183--190.

Coxhead, A., 2000, A New Academic Word List. TESOL Quarterly, 34(2), pp. 213-238. doi:10.2307/3587951

Crossley, S. A., Louwerse, M. M., McCarthy, P. M., & McNamara, D. S., 2007, A linguistic analysis of simplified and authentic texts. The Modern Language Journal, 91(1), 15-30.

Dela Rosa, K., Eskenazi, M., 2011, Impact of Word Sense Disambiguation on Ordering Dictionary Definitions in Vocabulary Learning Tutors, Proceedings of the 24th International FLAIRS Conference.

Dela Rosa, K., Parent, G.,Eskenazi, M., 2010, Multimodal learning of words: A study on the use of speech synthesis to reinforce written text in L2 language learning, Proceedings of the ISCA Workshop on Speech and Language Technology in Education (SLaTE 2010).

Geer, P., 2011, *GRE Verbal Workbook*. Hauppauge, NY: Barron's Educational Series.

Grace, C. A., 1998, Retention of Word Meanings Inferred from Context and Sentence-Level Translations: Implications for the Design of Beginning-Level CALL Software. *The Modern Language Journal, 82*, 533–544. doi: 10.1111/j.1540-4781.1998.tb05541.x

Hake, R., 1998, Interactive-engagement versus traditional methods: a six-thousand- student survey of mechanics test data for introductory physics courses. American Journal of Physics, 66, 64 – 74.

Heilman, M., Collins-Thompson, K., Callan, J. and Eskenazi, M., 2006, Classroom success of an Intelligent Tutoring System for lexical practice and reading comprehension. Proceedings of the Ninth International Conference on Spoken Language Processing (pp. 829-832). Pittsburgh, PA.

Heilman, M., Zhao, L., Pino, J., and Eskenazi, M., 2008, In Tetreault, T., Burstein, J. and De Felice, R. (Ed.) Retrieval of Reading Materials for Vocabulary and Reading Practice. Proceedings of the 3rd Workshop on Innovative Use of NLP for Building Educational Applications (pp.80-88), Columbus, OH: Association for Computational Linguistics. doi:10.3115/1631836.1631846

Inui, K., A. Fujita, T. Takahashi, R. Iida and T. Iwakura, 2003, Text simplification for reading assistance: a project note, Proceedings of the second international workshop on paraphrasing-volume 16, pages 9--16. Association for Computational Linguistics.

Jiang, N., 2000, Lexical representation and development in a second language. Applied Linguistics, 21(1), 47-77. doi: 10.1093/applin/21.1.47

Juffs, A., Wilson, L., Eskenazi, M., Callan, J., Brown, J., Collins-Thompson, K., Heilman, M., Pelletreau, T. and Sanders, J., 2006, Robust learning of vocabulary: investigating the relationship between learner behaviour and the acquisition of vocabulary. Paper presented at the 40th Annual TESOL Convention and Exhibit (TESOL 2006), Tampa Bay, FL.

Koehn, P., 2010, Statistical machine translation. Cambridge University Press.

Kroll, J. F. and Sunderman, G., 2003, Cognitive Processes in Second Language Learners and Bilinguals:

The Development of Lexical and Conceptual Representations. In C.J. Doughty and M. H. Long (Ed.), The Handbook of Second Language Acquisition. Oxford, UK: Blackwell Publishing Ltd,. doi: 10.1002/9780470756492.ch5

Leroy, G., Endicott, J.E., 2011, Term familiarity to indicate perceived and actual difficulty of text in medical digital libraries (ICADL 2011), Beijing.

Lin, Y., Saz, O., Eskenazi, M. (in review) Measuring the impact of translation on the accuracy and fluency of vocabulary acquisition of English

Medero, J., Ostendorf, M., 2011, Identifying Targets for Syntactic Simplification," Proc. ISCA SLaTE ITRW Workshop.

Oh, S-Y, 2008, Two types of input modification and EFL reading comprehension: simplification versus elaboration, TQD 2008, vol.35-1.

Perfetti, C.C., 2010, Decoding, vocabulary and comprehension: the golden triangle of reading skill, in M.G. McKeown and L. Kucan (Eds), Bringing reading researchers to life: essays in honor of Isabel Beck, pp. 291-303, New York: Guilford.

Petersen, S., Ostendorf, 2007, Text simplification for language learners: a corpus analysis, Proc ISCA SLaTE2007, Farmington PA

Prince, P., 1996, Second Language Vocabulary Learning: The Role of Context versus Translations as a Function of Proficiency. Modern Language Journal, 80(4), 478-493. doi:10.2307/329727

Taylor, W.L., 1953, Cloze procedure: a new tool for measuring readability, Journalism Quarterly, vol.30, pp. 415-433.

Walter, E., 2005, *Cambridge Advanced Learner's Dictionary, 2nd Edition.* Cambridge, UK: Cambridge University

Yano, Y., Long, M. H., & Ross, S., 1994, The effects of simplified and elaborated texts on foreign language reading comprehension, *Language Learning, 44*(2), 189-219.

Yatskar, M., Pang, B., Danescu-Niculescu-Mizil, C., Lee, L., 2010, For the sake of simplicity : unsupervised extraction of lexical simplifications from Wikipedia, Proc. NAACL 2010, p. 365-368.

Lexical Tightness and Text Complexity

Michael Flor **Beata Beigman Klebanov** **Kathleen M. Sheehan**

Educational Testing Service
Princeton, NJ, 08541, USA
{mflor,bbeigmanklebanov,ksheehan}@ets.org

Abstract

We present a computational notion of Lexical Tightness that measures global cohesion of content words in a text. Lexical tightness represents the degree to which a text tends to use words that are highly inter-associated in the language. We demonstrate the utility of this measure for estimating text complexity as measured by US school grade level designations of texts. Lexical tightness strongly correlates with grade level in a collection of expertly rated reading materials. Lexical tightness captures aspects of prose complexity that are not covered by classic readability indexes, especially for literary texts. We also present initial findings on the utility of this measure for automated estimation of complexity for poetry.

1 Introduction

Adequate estimation of text complexity has a long and rich history. Various readability metrics have been designed in the last 100 years (DuBay, 2004). Recent work on computational estimation of text complexity for school- and college-level texts includes (Vajjala and Meurers 2012; Graesser et al., 2011; Sheehan et al., 2010; Petersen and Ostendorf, 2009; Heilman et al., 2006). Several commercial systems were recently evaluated in the Race To The Top competition (Nelson et al., 2012) in relation to the US Common Core State Standards for instruction (CCSSI, 2010).

A variety of factors influence text complexity, including vocabulary, sentence structure, academic orientation, narrativity, cohesion, etc. (Hiebert, 2011) and corresponding features are utilized in automated systems of complexity evaluation (Vajjala and Meurers, 2012; Graesser et al., 2011; Sheehan et al., 2010).

We focus on text complexity levels expressed as US school grade level equivalents[1]. Our interest is in quantifying the differences among texts (essay-length reading passages) at different grade levels, for the purposes of automatically evaluating text complexity. The work described in this paper is part of an ongoing project that investigates novel features indicative of text complexity.

The paper is organized as follows. Section 2.1 presents our methodology for building word association profiles for texts. Section 2.2 defines the measure of lexical tightness (LT). Section 2.3 describes the datasets used in this study. Sections 3.1 and 3.2 present our study of the relationship between LT and text complexity. Section 3.3 describes application to poetry. Section 3.4 evaluates an improved measure (LTR). Section 4 reviews related work.

2 Methodology

2.1 Word-Association Profile

We define WAP_T – a word association profile of a text *T* – as the distribution of association values for all pairs of content words of text *T*, where the association values are estimated from a very large corpus of texts. In this work, WAP is purely illustrative, and sets the stage for lexical tightness.

[1] For age equivalents of grade levels see http://en.wikipedia.org/wiki/Educational_stage

There exists an extensive literature on the use of word-association measures for NLP, especially for detection of collocations (Pecina, 2010; Evert, 2008). The use of pointwise mutual information (PMI) with word-space models is noted in (Zhang et al., 2012; Baroni and Lenci, 2010; Mitchell and Lapata, 2008; Turney, 2001). We begin with PMI, and provide a modified measure in later sections.

To obtain comprehensive information about co-occurrence behavior of words in English, we build a first-order co-occurrence word-space model (Turney and Pantel, 2010; Baroni and Lenci, 2010). The model was generated from a corpus of texts of about 2.5 billion word tokens, counting non-directed co-occurrence in a paragraph, using no distance coefficients (Bullinaria and Levy, 2007). About 2 billion word tokens come from the Gigaword 2003 corpus (Graff and Cieri, 2003). Additional 500 million word tokens come from an in-house corpus containing texts from the genres of fiction and popular science. The matrix of 2.1x2.1 million word types and their co-occurrence frequencies, as well as single-word frequencies, is efficiently compressed using the TrendStream technology (Flor, 2013), resulting in a database file of 4.7GB. The same toolkit allows fast retrieval of word probabilities and statistical associations for pairs of words.[2]

In this study we use all content word tokens of a text. We use the OpenNLP tagger[3] to POS-tag a text and only take into account nouns, verbs, adjective and adverbs. We further apply a stop-list (see Appendix A) to filter out auxiliary verbs.

To illustrate why WAP is an interesting notion, consider this toy example: The texts "*The dog barked and wagged its tail*" vs. "*Green ideas sleep furiously*". Their matrices of pairwise word associations are presented in Table 1. For the first text, all the six content word pairs score above PMI=5.5. On the other hand, for "*Green ideas sleep furiously*", all the six content word pairs score below PMI=2.2. The first text puts together words that often go together in English, and this *might* be one of the reasons it seems easier to understand than the second text.

We use histograms to illustrate word-association profiles for real texts, containing hundreds of words. For a 60-bin histrogram spanning all obtained PMI values, the lowest bin contains pairs with PMI≤–5, the highest bin contains pairs with PMI>4.83, while the rest of the bins contain word pairs (a,b) with -5<PMI(a,b)≤4.83. Figure 1 presents WAP histograms for two real text samples, one for grade level 3 (age 8-9) and one for grade level 11 (age 16-17). We observe that the shape of distribution is normal-like. The distribution of GL3 text is shifted to the right – it contains more highly associated word-pairs than the text of GL11. In a separate study we investigated the properties of WAP distribution (Beigman-Klebanov and Flor, 2013). The normal-like shape turns out to be stable across a variety of texts.

The dog barked and wagged its tail:				
	dog	*barked*	*wagged*	*tail*
dog		*7.02*	*7.64*	*5.57*
barked			*9.18*	*5.95*
wagged				*9.45*
tail				
Green ideas sleep furiously:				
	green	*ideas*	*sleep*	*furiously*
green		*0.44*	*1.47*	*2.05*
ideas			*1.01*	*0.94*
sleep				*2.18*
furiously				

Table 1. Word association matrices (PMI values) for two illustrative examples.

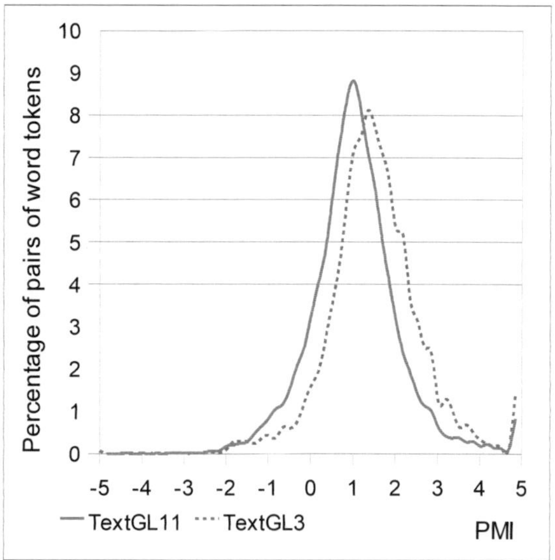

Figure 1. Word Association Profiles for two sample texts, showing 60-bin histograms with smoothed lines instead of bars. The last bin of the histogram contains all pairs with PMI>4.83, hence the uptick at PMI=5.

[2] The distributional word-space model includes counts for 2.1 million words and 1279 million word pairs (types). Association measures are computed on the fly.

[3] http://opennlp.apache.org

2.2 Lexical Tightness

In this section we consider how to derive a single measure to represent each text for further analyses. Given the stable normal-like shape of WAP, we use average (mean) value per text for further investigations. We experimented with several association measures.

Point-wise mutual information is defined as follows (Church and Hanks, 1990):

$$\text{PMI} = \log_2 \frac{p(a,b)}{p(a)\,p(b)}$$

Normalized PMI (Bouma, 2009):

$$\text{NPMI} = \left(\log_2 \frac{p(a,b)}{p(a)p(b)} \right) \Big/ - \log_2 p(a,b)$$

Unlike the standard PMI (Manning and Schütze, 1999), NPMI has the property that its values are mostly constrained in the range {-1,1}, it is less influenced by rare extreme values, which is convenient for summing values over multiple pairs of words. Additional experiments on our data have shown that ignoring negative NPMI values[4] works best. Thus, we define Positive Normalized PMI (PNPMI) for a pair of words *a* and *b* as follows:

$$\text{PNPMI}(a,b) \begin{cases} = \text{NPMI}(a,b) & \text{if NPMI}(a,b)>0 \\ = 0 & \text{if NPMI}(a,b)\le 0 \\ & \text{or if database has no data for co-occurrence of } a \text{ and } b.^5 \end{cases}$$

We define **Lexical Tightness** (**LT**) of a text as the mean value of PNPMI for all pairs of content-word tokens in a text. Thus, if a text has *N* words, and after filtering we remain with *K* content words, the total number of pairs is *K*(K-1)/2*.

Lexical tightness represents the degree to which a text tends to use words that are highly inter-associated in the language. We conjecture that lexically tight texts (with higher values of LT) are easier to read and would thus correspond to lower grade levels.

[4] Ignoring negative values is described by Bullinaria and Levy (2007), also Mohammad and Hirst (2006).

[5] In our text collection, the average percentage of word-pairs not found in database is 5.5% per text.

2.3 Datasets

Our data consists of two sets of passages. The first set consists of 1012 passages (636K words) – reading materials that were used in various tests in state and national assessment frameworks in the USA. Part of this set is taken from Sheehan et al. (2007) (from testing programs and US state departments of education), and part was taken from the Standardized State Test Passages set of the Race To The Top (RTT) competition (Nelson et al., 2012). A distinguishing feature of this dataset is that the exact grade level specification was available for each text. Table 2 provides the breakdown by grade and genre. Text length in this set ranged between 27 and 2848 words, with average 629 words. Average text length in the literary subset was 689 words and in the informational subset 560 words.

Grade Level	Genre: Inf	Lit	Other	Total
1	2	4	1	7
2	2	4	3	9
3	49	63	10	122
4	54	77	8	139
5	47	48	15	110
6	44	43	6	93
7	39	61	6	106
8	73	66	19	158
9	25	25	3	53
10	29	52	2	83
11	18	25	0	43
12	47	20	22	89
Total	429	488	95	1012

Table 2. Counts of texts by grade level and genre, set #1

Grade Band	GL	Genre: Inf	Lit	Other	Total
2–3	2.5	6	10	4	20
4–5	4.5	16	10	4	30
6–8	7	12	16	13	41
9–10	9.5	12	10	17	39
11+	11.5	8	10	20	38
Total		54	56	58	168

Table 3. Counts of texts by grade band and genre, for dataset #2. GL specifies our grade level designation.

The second dataset comprises 168 texts (80.8K word tokens) from Appendix B of the Common Core State Standards (CCSSI, 2010)[6], not includ-

[6] www.corestandards.org/assets/Appendix_B.pdf

ing poetry items. Exact grade level designations are not available for this set, rather the texts are classified into grade bands, as established by expert instructors (Nelson et al., 2012). Table 3 provides the breakdown by grade and genre. Text length in this set ranged between 99 and 2073 words, with average 481 words. Average text length in the literary subset was 455 words and in the informational subset 373 words.

Our collection is not very large in terms of typical datasets used in NLP research. However, it has two unique facets: grading and genres. Rather than having grade-ranges, set #1 has exact grade designations for each text. Moreover, these were rated by educational experts and used in state and nationwide testing programs.

Previous research has emphasized the importance of genre effects for predicting readability and complexity (Sheehan et al., 2008) and for text adaptation (Fountas and Pinnell, 2001). For all texts in our collection, genre designations (informational, literary, or 'other') were provided by expert human judges (we used the designations that were prepared for the RTT competition, Nelson et al., 2012). The 'other' category included texts that were somewhere in between literary and informational (e.g. biographies), as well as speeches, schedules, and manuals.

3 Results

3.1 Lexical Tightness and Grade Level

Correlations of lexical tightness with grade level are shown in Table 4, for sets 1 and 2, the combined set and for literary and informational subsets.

Our first finding is that lexical tightness has considerable and statistically significant correlation with grade level, in each dataset, in the combined dataset and for the specific subsets. Notably the correlation between lexical tightness and grade level is negative. Texts of higher grade levels are lexically less tight, as predicted.

Although in these datasets grade level is moderately correlated with text length, lexical tightness remains considerably and significantly correlated with grade level even after removing the influence of correlations with text length.

Our second finding is that lexical tightness has a stronger correlation with grade level for the subset of literary texts (r=-0.610) than for informational texts (r=-0.499) in set #1. A similar pattern exists for set #2.

Figure 2 shows the average LT for each grade level, for texts of set #1. As the grade level increases, average lexical tightness values decrease consistently, especially for informational and literary texts. There are two 'outliers'. Informational texts for grade 12 show a sudden increase in lexical tightness. Also, for genre 'other', grades 9,10,11 are underepresented (see Table 2).

Subset	N	Correlation GL&length	Correlation GL&LT	Partial Correlation GL&LT
Set #1				
All	1012	0.362	-0.546	-0.472
Inf	429	0.396	-0.499	-0.404
Lit	488	0.408	-0.610	-0.549
Set #2 (Common Core)				
All	168	0.360	-0.441	-0.373
Inf	54	0.406	-0.313	-0.347
Lit	56	0.251	-0.546	-0.505
Combined set				
All	1180	0.339	-0.528	-0.462
Inf	483	0.386	-0.472	-0.369
Lit	544	0.374	-0.601	-0.545

Table 4. Correlations of grade level (GL) with text length and lexical tightness (LT). Partial correlation GL&LT controls for text length. All correlations are significant with $p<0.04$.

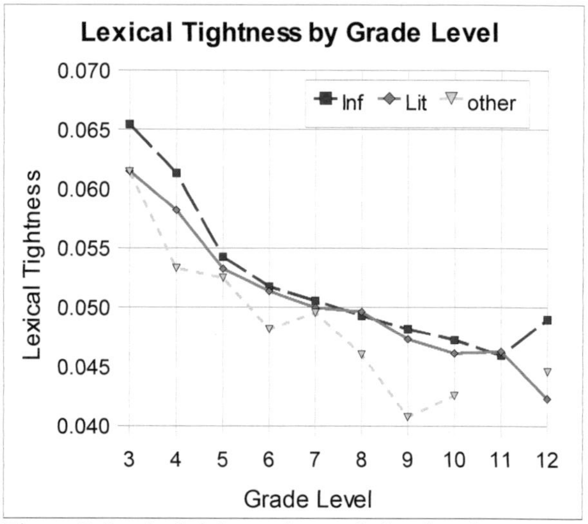

Figure 2. Lexical tighness by grade level and genre, for texts of grades 3-12 in dataset #1.

Figure 3 shows the average LT for each grade band, for texts of set #2. Here as well, decrease of lexical tightness is evident with increase of grade level. In this small set, informational texts show a relatively smooth decrease of LT, while literary texts show a sharp decrease of LT in transition from grade band 4-5 (4.5) to grade band 6-8 (7). Texts labelled as 'other' genre in set #2 are generally less 'tight' than literary or informational. Also for 'other' genre, bands 7-8, 9-10 and 11-12 have equal lexical tighness.

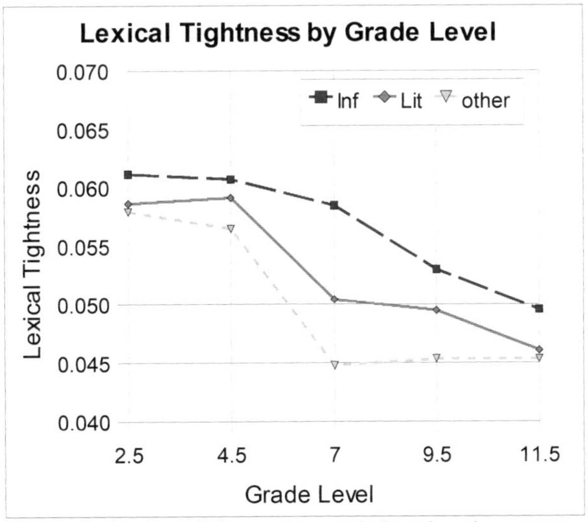

Figure 3. Lexical tighness by grade band and genre, for texts in dataset #2 (CommonCore).

3.2 Grade Level and Readability Indexes

We have also calculated readability indexes for each passage in sets 1 and 2. We used well known readability formulae: Flesch-Kincaid Grade Level (FKGL: Kincaid et al., 1975), Flesch Reading Ease (FRE: Flesch, 1948), Gunning-Fog Index (GFI: Gunning, 1952[7]), Coleman Liau Index (CLI: Coleman and Liau, 1975) and Automated Readability Index (ARI: Senter and Smith, 1967). All of them are based on measuring the length of words (in letters or syllables) and length of sentences (mean number of words). For our collection, we also computed the average sentence length (avgSL, as word count), average word frequency[8] (avgWF – over all words), and average word frequency for only content words (avgWFCW). Results are shown in Table 5.

Word frequency has quite low correlation with grade level in both datasets. Readability indexes have a strong and consistent correlation with grade level. For dataset #1, readability indexes have much stronger correlation with grade level for informational texts (|*r*| between 0.7 and 0.81) as compared to literary texts (|*r*| between 0.53 and 0.68), and a similar pattern is seen for dataset #2, with overall lower correlation.

The correlation of Flesch-Kincaid (FKGL) values with LT are *r*=-0.444 for set #1, *r*=-0.499 for the informational subset and *r*=-0.541 for literary subset. The correlation is *r*=-0.182 in set #2.

	All	Inf	Lit
Set #1			
N (texts):	1012	429	488
FKGL	0.705	0.807	0.673
FRE	-0.658	-0.797	-0.629
GFI	0.701	0.810	0.673
CLI	0.537	0.722	0.537
ARI	0.670	0.784	0.653
avgSL	0.667	0.705	0.630
avgWF	0.205	0.128	0.249
avgWFCW	*0.039*	*-0.039*	0.095
Set #2 (Common Core)			
N (texts):	168	54	56
FKGL	0.487	0.670	0.312
FRE[9]	-0.503	-0.586	-0.398
GFI	0.493	0.622	0.356
CLI	0.430	0.457	0.440
ARI	0.458	0.658	0.298
avgSL	0.407	0.701	*0.203*
avgWF	*0.100*	0.234	*-0.109*
avgWFCW	0.156	*-0.053*	*-0.038*

Table 5. Correlations of grade level with readability formulae and word frequency. All correlations apart from the italicized ones are significant with p<0.05. Abbreviations are explained in the text.

3.3 Lexical Tightness and Readability Indexes

To evaluate the usefulness of LT in predicting grade level of passages, we estimate, using dataset #1, a linear regression model where the grade level is a dependent variable and Flesch-Kincaid score and lexical tightness are the two independent variables (features). First, we checked whether regression model improves over FKGL in the training set (#1). Then, we tested the regression model estimated on 1012 texts of set #1, on 168 texts of set #2.

The results of the regression model on 1012 texts of set #1 (R^2=0.565, F(2,1009)=655.85,

[7] Using the modern formula, as referenced at http://en.wikipedia.org/wiki/Fog_Index

[8] For word frequency we use the unigrams data from the Google Web1T collection (Brants and Franz, 2006).

[9] Flesch Reading Ease formula is inversely related to grade level, hence the negative correlations.

p<0.0001) indicate that the amount of explained variance in the grade levels, as measured by the adjusted R^2 of the model, improved from 0.497 (with FKGL alone, *multiple* r=0.705) to 0.564 (FKGL with LT, r=0.752), that is an absolute improvement of 6.7%, and a relative improvement of 13.5%.

A separate regression model was estimated on the informational texts of dataset #1. The result (R^2=0.664, F(2,426)=420.3, p<0.0001) reveals that adjusted R^2 of the model improved from 0.651 (with FKGL alone, r=0.807) to 0.663 (FKGL with LT, r=0.815). Similarly, a regression model was estimated on the literary texts of set #1. The result (R^2=0.522, F(2,485)=264.6, p<0.0001) reveals that adjusted R^2 of the model improved from .453 (with FKGL alone, r=0.673) to 0.520 (FKGL with LT, r=0.722). We observe that Flesch-Kincaid formula works well on informational texts, better than on literary texts; while lexical tightness correlates with grade level in the literary texts better than it does in the informational texts. Thus, for informational texts, adding LT to FKGL provides a small (1.2%) but statistically significant improvement for predicting GL. For literary texts, LT provides a considerable improvement (explaining additional 6.3% in the variance).

We use the regression model (FKGL & LT) estimated on the 1012 texts of set #1 and test it on 168 texts of set #2. In dataset #2, FKGL alone correlates with grade level with r=0.487, and the estimated regression equation achieves correlation of r=0.574 (the difference between correlation coefficients is statistically significant[10], p<0.001). The amount of explained variance rises from 23.7% to 33%, an almost 10% improvement in absolute scores, and 39% relative improvement over FKGL readability index alone.

3.4 Analyzing Poetry

Since poetry is often included in school curricula, automated estimation of poem complexity can be useful. Poetry is notoriously hard to analyze computationally. Many poems do not adhere to standard punctuation conventions, have peculiar sentence structure (if sentence boundaries are indicated at all). However, poems can be tackled with bag-of-words approaches.

We have collected 66 poems from Appendix B of the Common Core State Standards (CCSSI, 2010). Just as other materials from that source, the poems are classified into grade bands, as established by expert instructors. Table 6 provides the breakdown by grade band. Text length in this set ranges between 21 and 1100 words, the average is 182, total word count is 12,030.

Grade Band	GL	N (texts)
K-1	1	12
2–3	2.5	15
4–5	4.5	9
6–8	7	11
9–10	9.5	7
11+	11.5	12
Total		66

Table 6. Counts of poems by grade band, from Common Core Appendix B.
GL specifies our grade level designation.

We computed lexical tightness for all 66 poems using the same procedure as for the two larger text collections. For computing correlations, texts from each grade band where assigned grade level as listed in Table 6. For the poetry dataset, LT has rather low correlation with grade level, r=-0.271 (p<0.002). Text length correlation with GL is r=0.218 (p<0.04). Correlation of LT and text length is r=-0.261 (p<0.02). Partial correlation of LT and GL, controlling for text length, is r=-0.227 and only almost significant (p=0.069). In this dataset, the correlation of Flesch-Kincaid index (FKGL) with GL is r=0.291 (p<0.003) and Flesch Reading Ease (FRE) has a stronger correlation, r=-0.335 (p<0.003).

On examining some of the poems, we noted that the LT measure does not assign enough importance to recurrence of words within a text. For example, PNPMI(*voice*, *voice*) is 0.208, while the ceiling value is 1.0. We modify the LT measure in the following way. Revised Association Score (RAS) for two words a and b:

$$\mathrm{RAS}(a,b) \begin{cases} =1.0 & \text{if } a=b \text{ (token repetition)} \\ =0.9 & \text{if } a \text{ and } b \text{ are inflectional variants of same lemma} \\ =\mathrm{PNPMI}(a,b) & \text{otherwise} \end{cases}$$

Revised Lexical Tightness (**LTR**) for a text is average of RAS scores for all accepted word pairs in the text (same filtering as before).

[10]Non-independent correlations test, McNemar (1955), p.148.

For the set of 66 poems, LTR moderately correlates with grade level r=-0.353 ($p<0.002$). LTR correlates with text length r=0.28 ($p<0.02$). Partial correlation of LTR and GL, controlling for text length, is r=-0.312 ($p<0.012$). This suggests that the revised measure captures some aspect of complexity of the poems.

We re-estimated the regression model, using FRE readability and LTR, on all 1012 texts of set #1. We then applied this model for prediction of grade levels in the set of 66 poems. The model achieves a solid correlation with grade level, ***r*=0.447** ($p<0.0001$).

3.5 Revisiting Prose

We revisit the analysis of our two main datasets, set #1 and #2, using the revised lexical tightness measure LTR. Table 7 presents correlations of grade level with LT and LTR measures. Evidently, in each case LTR achieves better correlations.

Subset	N	Correlation GL&LT	Correlation GL&LTR
Set #1			
All	1012	-0.546	-0.605
Inf	429	-0.499	-0.561
Lit	488	-0.610	-0.659
Set #2 (Common Core)			
All	168	-0.441	-0.492
Inf	54	-0.310	-0.336
Lit	56	-0.546	-0.662
Combined set			
All	1180	-0.528	-0.587
Inf	483	-0.472	-0.531
Lit	544	-0.601	-0.655

Table 7. Pearson correlations of grade level (GL) with lexical tightness (LT) and revised lexical tightness (LTR). All correlations are significant with $p<0.04$.

We re-estimated a linear regression model using the grade level as a dependent variable and Flesch-Kincaid score (FKGL) and LTR as the two independent variables. The results of regression model on 1012 texts of dataset #1, R^2=0.583, $F(2,1009)$=706.07, $p<0.0001$, indicate that the amount of explained variance in the grade levels, as measured by the adjusted R^2 of the model, improved from 0.497 (with FKGL alone, r=0.705) to 0.582 (FKGL with LTR, r=0.764), that is absolute improvement of 8.5%. For comparison, the regression model with LT explained 0.564 of the variance, with 6.7% improvement over FKGL alone.

We re-estimated separate regression models for informational and literary subsets of set #1. For informational texts, the model has R^2=0.667, $F(2,426)$=426.8, $p<0.0001$, R^2 improving from 0.651 (with FKGL alone, r=0.807) to adjusted R^2 0.666 (FKGL with LTR, r=0.817). Regression model with LT brought an improvement of 1.2%, the model with LTR provides 1.5%.

A regression model was estimated on the literary texts of dataset #1. The result (R^2=0.560, $F(2,485)$=308.5, $p<0.0001$) reveals that adjusted R^2 of the model rose from .453 (with FKGL alone, r=0.673) to 0.558 (FKGL with LT, r=0.748), that is 10.5% absolute improvement. For comparison, LT brought 6.3% improvement. As with the original LT measure, LTR provides the bulk of improvement for evaluation of literary texts.

The regression model (FKGL with LTR), estimated on all 1012 texts of set #1, is tested on 168 texts of set #2. In set #2, FKGL alone correlates with grade level with r=0.487, and the prediction formula achieves correlation of r=0.585 (the difference between correlation coefficients is statistically significant, $p<0.001$). The amount of explained variance rises from 23.7% to 34.3%, that is 10.6% absolute improvement. Even better result of predicting grade level in set #2 is achieved using a regression model of Flesch Readability Ease (FRE) and LTR, estimated on all 1012 texts of set #1. This model achieves correlation of r=0.616 ($p<0.0001$) on the 168 texts of set #2, explaining 37.9% of the variance.

For complexity estimation, in both proze and poetry, LTR is more effective than simple LT.

4 Related Work

Traditional readability formulae use a small number of surface features, such as the average sentence length (a proxy for syntactic complexity) and the average word length in syllables or characters (a proxy to vocabulary difficulty). Such features are considered linguistically shallow, but they are surprisingly effective and are still widely used (DuBay, 2004; Štajner et al., 2012). The formulae or their features are incorporated in modern readability classification systems (Vajjala and Meurers, 2012; Sheehan et al., 2010; Petersen and Ostendorf, 2009).

Developments in computational linguistics enabled inclusion of multiple features for capturing various manifestations of text-related readability. Peterson and Ostendorf (2009) compute a variety of features: vocabulary/lexical (including the classic 'syllables per word'), parse features, including average parse-tree height, noun-phrase count, verb-phrase count and average count of subordinated clauses. They use machine learning to train classifiers for direct prediction of grade level. Vajjala and Meurers (2012) also use machine learning, with a wide variety of features, including classic features, parse features, and features motivated from studies on second language acquisition, such as Lexical Density and Type-Token Ratio. Word frequency and its derivations, such as proportion of rare words, are utilized in many models of complexity (Graesser et al., 2011; Sheehan et al, 2010; Stenner et al., 2006; Collins-Thompson and Callan, 2004).

Inspired by psycholinguistic research, two systems have explicitly set to measure textual cohesion for estimations of readability and complexity: Coh-Metrix (Graesser et al., 2011) and SourceRater (Sheehan et al., 2010). One notion of cohesion involved in those two systems is *lexical cohesion* – the amount of lexically/semantically related words in a text. Some amount of local lexical cohesion can be measured via stem overlap of adjacent sentences, with averaging of such metric per text (McNamara et al., 2010). However, Sheehan et al. (submitted) demonstrated that such measure is not well correlated with grade levels.

Perhaps closest to our present study is work reported in Foltz et al. (1998) and McNamara et al. (2010). These studies used Latent Semantic Analysis, which reflects second order co-occurrence associative relations, to characterize levels of lexical similarity for pairs of adjacent sentences within paragraphs, and for all possible pairs of sentences within paragraphs. McNamara et al. have shown success in distinguishing lower and higher cohesion versions of the same text, but have not shown whether that approach systematically applies for different texts and across grade levels.

Our study is a first demonstration that a measure of lexical cohesion based on word-associations, and computed globally for the whole text, is an indicative feature that varies systematically across grade levels.

In the theoretical tradition, our work is closest in spirit to Michael Hoey's theory of lexical priming (Hoey, 2005, 1991), positing that users of language internalize patterns of word co-occurrence and use them in reading, as well as when creating their own texts. We suggest that such patterns become richer with age and education, beginning with the most tight patterns at early age.

5 Conclusions

In this paper we defined a novel computational measure, lexical tightness. It represents the degree to which a text tends to use words that are highly inter-associated in the language. We interpret lexical tightness as a measure of intra-text global cohesion.

This study presented the relationship between lexical tightness and text complexity, using two datasets of reading materials (1180 texts in total), with expert-assigned grade levels. Lexical tightness has a significant correlation with grade levels: about -0.6 overall. The correlation is negative: texts for lower grades are lexically tight, they use a higher proportion of mildly and strongly inter-associated words; texts for higher grades are less tight, they use a lesser amount of inter-associated words. The correlation of lexical tightness with grade level is stronger for texts of the literary genre (fiction and stories) than for text belonging to informational genre (expositional).

While lexical tightness is moderately correlated with readability indexes, it also captures some aspects of prose complexity that are not covered by classic readability indexes, especially for literary texts. Regression analyses on a training set have shown that lexical tightness adds between 6.7% and 8.5% of explained grade level variance on top of the best readability formula. The utility of lexical tightness was confirmed by testing the regression formula on a held out set of texts.

Lexical tightness is also moderately correlated with grade level (-0.353) in a small set of poems. In the same set, Flesch Reading Ease readability formula correlates with grade level at -0.335. A regression model using that formula and lexical tightness achieves correlation of 0.447 with grade level. Thus we have shown that lexical tightness has good potential for analysis of poetry.

In future work, we intend to a) evaluate on larger datasets, and b) integrate lexical tightness with other features used for estimation of readability. We also intend to use this or a related measure for evaluation of writing quality.

References

Baroni M. and Lenci A. 2010. Distributional Memory: A General Framework for Corpus-Based Semantics. *Computational Linguistics*, 36(4):673-721.

Beigman-Klebanov B. and Flor M. 2013. Word Association Profiles and their Use for Automated Scoring of Essays. To appear in *Proceedings of the 51th Annual Meeting of the Association for Computational Linguistics*, ACL 2013.

Bouma G. 2009. Normalized (Pointwise) Mutual Information in Collocation Extraction. In: Chiarcos, Eckart de Castilho & Stede (eds), *From Form to Meaning: Processing Texts Automatically, Proceedings of the Biennial GSCL Conference 2009*, 31–40, Gunter Narr Verlag: Tübingen.

Brants T. and Franz A. 2006. "Web 1T 5-gram Version 1". LDC2006T13. Linguistic Data Consortium, Philadelphia, PA.

Bullinaria J. and Levy J. 2007. Extracting semantic representations from word co-occurrence statistics: A computational study. *Behavior Research Methods*, 39:510–526.

Church K. and Hanks P. 1990. Word association norms, mutual information and lexicography. *Computational Linguistics*, 16(1):22–29.

Coleman, M. and Liau, T. L. 1975. A computer readability formula designed for machine scoring. *Journal of Applied Psychology*, 60:283-284.

Collins-Thompson K. and Callan J. 2004. A language modeling approach to predicting reading difficulty. *Proceedings of HLT / NAACL 2004*, Boston, USA.

Common Core State Standards Initiative (CCSSI) 2010. Common core state standards for English language arts & literacy in history/social studies, science and technical subjects. Washington, DC: CCSSO & National Governors Association. http://www.corestandards.org/ELA-Literacy

DuBay W.H. 2004. The principles of readability. Impact Information: Costa Mesa, CA. http://www.impact-information.com/impactinfo/readability02.pdf

Evert S. 2008. Corpora and collocations. In A. Lüdeling and M. Kytö (eds.), *Corpus Linguistics: An International Handbook*, article 58. Mouton de Gruyter: Berlin.

Flesch R. 1948. A new readability yardstick. *Journal of Applied Psychology*, 32:221-233.

Flor M. 2013. A fast and flexible architecture for very large word n-gram datasets. *Natural Language Engineering*, 19(1):61-93.

Foltz P.W., Kintsch W., and Landauer T.K. 1998. The measurement of textual coherence with Latent Semantic Analysis. *Discourse Processes*, 25:285-307.

Fountas I. and Pinnell G.S. 2001. Guiding Readers and Writers, Grades 3–6. Heinemann, Portsmouth, NH.

Graesser, A.C., McNamara, D.S., and Kulikowich, J.M. Coh-Metrix: Providing Multilevel Analyses of Text Characteristics. *Educational Researcher*, 40(5): 223–234.

Graff, D. and Cieri, C. 2003. English Gigaword. LDC2003T05. Linguistic Data Consortium, Philadelphia, PA.

Gunning R. 1952. *The technique of clear writing*. McGraw-Hill: New York.

Heilman, M., Collins-Thompson, K., Callan, J. and Eskenazi, M. 2006. Classroom success of an intelligent tutoring system for lexical practice and reading comprehension. In *Proceedings of the Ninth International Conference on Spoken Language Processing*, Pittsburgh, PA.

Hiebert, E.H. 2011. *Using multiple sources of information in establishing text complexity*. Reading Research Report 11.03. TextProject Inc., Santa Cruz, CA.

Hoey M. 1991. *Patterns of Lexis in Text*. Oxford University Press.

Hoey M. 2005. *Lexical Priming: A new theory of words and language*. Routledge, London.

Kincaid J.P., Fishburne R.P. Jr, Rogers R.L., and Chissom B.S. 1975. *Derivation of new readability formulas for Navy enlisted personnel*. Research Branch Report 8-75, Millington, TN: Naval Technical Training, U.S. Naval Air Station, Memphis, TN.

Manning, C. and Schütze H. 1999. *Foundations of Statistical Natural Language Processing*. MIT Press, Cambridge, MA.

McNamara, D.S., Louwerse, M.M., McCarthy, P.M. and Graesser A.C. 2010. Coh-metrix: Capturing linguistic features of cohesion. *Discourse Processes*, 47:292-330.

McNemar, Q. 1955. *Psychological Statistics*. New York, John Wiley & Sons.

Mitchell J. and Lapata M. 2008. Vector-based models of semantic composition. In *Proceedings of the 46th Annual Meeting of the Association for Computational Linguistics*, 236–244, Columbus, OH.

Mohammad S. and Hirst G. 2006. Distributional Measures of Concept-Distance: A Task-oriented Evaluation. In *Proceedings of the 2006 Conference on Empirical Methods in Natural Language Processing* (EMNLP 2006), 35–43.

Nelson J., Perfetti C., Liben D., and Liben M. 2012. Measures of Text Difficulty: Testing their Predictive Value for Grade Levels and Student Performance. Student Achievement Partners. Available from http://www.ccsso.org/Documents/2012/Measures%20ofText%20Difficulty_final.2012.pdf

Pecina P. 2010. Lexical association measures and collocation extraction. *Language Resources & Evaluation*, 44:137–158.

Petersen S.E. and Ostendorf M. 2009. A machine learning approach to reading level assessment. *Computer Speech and Language*, 23: 89–109.

Senter R.J. and Smith E.A. 1967. *Automated Readability Index*. Report AMRL-TR-6620. Wright-Patterson Air Force Base, USA.

Sheehan K.M., Kostin I., Napolitano D., and Flor M. TextEvaluator: Helping Teachers and Test Developers Select Texts for Use in Instruction and Assessment. Submitted to *The Elementary School Journal* (Special Issue: Text Complexity).

Sheehan K.M., Kostin I., Futagi Y., and Flor M. 2010. Generating automated text complexity classifications that are aligned with targeted text complexity standards. (ETS RR-10-28). ETS, Princeton, NJ.

Sheehan K.M., Kostin I., and Futagi Y. 2008. When do standard approaches for measuring vocabulary difficulty, syntactic complexity and referential cohesion yield biased estimates of text difficulty? In B.C. Love, K. McRae, & V.M. Sloutsky (eds.), *Proceedings of the 30th Annual Conference of the Cognitive Science Society*, Washington DC.

Sheehan K.M., Kostin I., and Futagi Y. 2007. SourceFinder: A construct-driven approach for locating appropriately targeted reading comprehension source texts. In *Proceedings of the 2007 workshop of the International Speech Communication Association*, Special Interest Group on Speech and Language Technology in Education, Farmington, PA.

Štajner S., Evans R., Orăsan C., and Mitkov R. 2012. What Can Readability Measures Really Tell Us About Text Complexity? In proceedings of workshop on *Natural Language Processing for Improving Textual Accessibility* (NLP4ITA 2012), 14-22.

Stenner A.J., Burdick H., Sanford E., and Burdick D. 2006. How accurate are Lexile text measures? *Journal of Applied Measurement*, 7(3):307-322.

Turney P.D. 2001. Mining the Web for Synonyms: PMI-IR versus LSA on TOEFL. In proceedings of *European Conference on Machine Learning*, 491–502, Freiburg, Germany.

Turney P.D. and Pantel P. 2010. From Frequency to Meaning: Vector Space Models of Semantics. *Journal of Artificial Intelligence Research*, 37:141-188.

Vajjala S. and Meurers D. 2012. On Improving the Accuracy of Readability Classification using Insights from Second Language Acquisition. In proceedings of *The 7th Workshop on the Innovative Use of NLP for Building Educational Applications*, (BEA-7), 163–173, ACL.

Zhang Z., Gentile A.L., Ciravegna F. 2012. Recent advances in methods of lexical semantic relatedness – a survey. *Natural Language Engineering*, DOI: http://dx.doi.org/10.1017/S1351324912000125

Appendix A

The list of stopwords utilized in this study:

a, an, the, at, as, by, for, from, in, on, of, off, up, to, out, over, if, then, than, with, have, had, has, can, could, do, did, does, be, am, are, is, was, were, would, will, it, this, that, no, not, yes, but, all, and, or, any, so, every, we, us, you, also, s

Note that most of these words would be excluded by POS filtering. However, the full stop list was applied anyway.

A System for the Simplification of Numerical Expressions at Different Levels of Understandability

Susana Bautista, Raquel Hervás, Pablo Gervás
Universidad Complutense de Madrid
Prof. José García Santesmases
Madrid, Spain
{subautis,raquelhb}@fdi.ucm.es
pgervas@sip.ucm.es

Richard Power, Sandra Williams
Department of Computing,
The Open University
Milton Keynes,
MK76AA, UK
r.power@open.ac.uk
s.h.williams@open.ac.uk

Abstract

The purpose of this paper is to motivate and describe a system that simplifies numerical expression in texts, along with an evaluation study in which experts in numeracy and literacy assessed the outputs of this system. We have worked with a collection of newspaper articles with a significant number of numerical expressions. The results are discussed in comparison to conclusions obtained from a prior empirical survey.

1 Introduction

A surprisingly large number of people have limited access to information because of poor literacy. The most recent surveys of literacy in the United Kingdom reveal that 7 million adults in England cannot locate the reference page for plumbers if given the Yellow Pages alphabetical index. This means that one in five adults has less literacy than the expected literacy in an 11-year-old child (Jama and Dugdale, 2010; Williams et al., 2003a; Christina and Jonathan, 2010). Additionally, almost 24 million adults in the U.K. have insufficient numeracy skills to perform simple everyday tasks such as paying household bills and understanding wage slips. They would be unable to achieve grade C in the GCSE maths examination for 16-year-old school children (Williams et al., 2003a).

"The Standard Rules on the Equalization of Opportunities for Persons with Disabilities" by United Nations (1994) state that all public information services and documents should be accessible in such a way that they could be easily understood. If we focus on numerical information, nowadays, a large percentage of information expressed in daily news or reports comes in the form of numerical expressions (economic statistics, demography data, etc) but many people have problems understanding the more complex expressions. In the text simplification process, different tasks are carried out: replacing difficult words, splitting sentences, etc., and the simplification of numerical expressions is one of them.

A possible approach to solve this important social problem of making numerical information accessible is to rewrite difficult numerical expressions using alternative wordings that are easier to understand. For example, the original sentence, "25.9% scored A grades" could be rewritten by "Around 26% scored A grades". In our study we define a "numerical expression" as a phrase that presents a quantity, sometimes modified by a numerical hedge as in these examples: 'less than a quarter' or 'about 98%'. Such an approach would require a set of rewriting strategies yielding expressions that are linguistically correct, easier to understand than the original, and as close as possible to the original meaning. Some loss of precision could have positive advantages for numerate people as well as less numerate. In rewriting, hedges play also an important role. For example, '50.9%' could be rewritten as 'about a half' using the hedge 'about'. In this kind of simplification, hedges indicate that the original number has been approximated and, in some cases, also the direction of the approximation.

This paper presents a system developed for automated simplification of numerical expressions. Experts in simplification tasks are asked to validate the simplifications done automatically. The system is evaluated and the results are discussed against conclusions obtained from previous empirical survey.

2 Previous work

Text simplification, a relative new task in Natural Language Processing, has been directed mainly at syntactic constructions and lexical choices that some readers find difficult, such as long sentences, passives, coordinate and subordinate clauses, abstract words, low frequency words, and abbreviations.

The rule-based paradigm has been used in the implementation of some systems for text simplification, each one focusing on a variety of readers (with poor literacy, aphasia, etc) (Chandrasekar et al., 1996; Siddharthan, 2003; Jr. et al., 2009; Bautista et al., 2009).

The transformation of texts into easy-to-read versions can also be phrased as a translation problem between two different subsets of language: the original and the easy-to-read version. Corpus-based systems can learn from corpora the simplification operations and also the required degree of simplification for a given task (Daelemans et al., 2004; Petersen and Ostendorf, 2007; Gasperin et al., 2009).

A variety of simplification techniques have been used, substituting common words for uncommon words (Devlin and Tait, 1998), activating passive sentences and resolving references (Canning, 2000), reducing multiple-clause sentences to single-clause sentences (Chandrasekar and Srinivas, 1997; Canning, 2000; Siddharthan, 2002) and making appropriate choices at the discourse level (Williams et al., 2003b). Khan et at. (2008) studied the tradeoff between brevity and clarity in the context of generating referring expressions. Other researchers have focused on the generation of readable texts for readers with low basic skills (Williams and Reiter, 2005), and for teaching foreign languages (Petersen and Ostendorf, 2007).

Previous work on numerical expressions has studied the treatment of numerical information in different areas like health (Peters et al., 2007), forecast (Dieckmann et al., 2009), representation of probabilistic information (Bisantz et al., 2005) or vague information (Mishra et al., 2011). In the NUMGEN project (Williams and Power, 2009), a corpus of numerical expressions was collected and a formal model for planning specifications for proportions (numbers between 0 and 1) was developed. The underlying theory and the design of the working program are described in (Power and Williams, 2012).

3 Experimental identification of simplification strategies for numerical information

In order to analyze different simplification strategies for numerical expressions, first we have to study the mathematical complexity of the expressions. Expressions can be classified and a level of difficulty can be assigned. A study about the simplification strategies selected by experts to simplify numerical expressions expressed as decimal percentages in a corpus was carried out in Bautista et al. (2011b). Other important aspect of the simplification task is the use of hedges to simplify numerical expressions in the text. A study was performed in Bautista et al. (2011a) to analyze the use of hedges in the simplification process. This study was done with experts in simplification tasks. A set of sentences with numerical expressions were presented and they had to rewrite the numerical expressions following some rules. Several hypotheses were expressed and analyzed to understand experts' preferences on simplification strategies and use of hedges to simplify numerical expressions in the text. The main conclusions from the study were:

Conclusion 1: When experts choose expressions for readers with low numeracy, they tend to prefer round or common values to precise values. For example, halves, thirds and quarters are usually preferred to eighths or similar, and expressions like *N in 10* or *N in 100* are chosen instead of *N in 36*.

Conclusion 2: The value of the original proportion influences the choice of simplification strategies (fractions, ratios, percentages). With values in the central range (say 0.2 to 0.8 in a 0.0 to 1.0 scale) and values at the extreme ranges (say 0.0-0.2 and 0.8-1.0) favoring different strategies.

Conclusion 3: When writers choose numerical expressions for readers with low numeracy, they only use hedges if they are losing precision.

4 A system for adapting numerical expressions

In this first prototype, only numerical expressions defined as percentages are adapted. From an input text, the percentage numerical expressions are detected, a target level of difficulty is chosen and the simplified version of the text is generated by replacing the original numerical expression with the adapted expression.

4.1 Numerical expression

A numerical expression consists of: (1) a numerical value, a quantity which may be expressed with digits or with words; (2) an optional unit accompanying the quantity (euro, miles, ...); and (3) an optional numerical hedge modifier (around, less than, ...). Some examples of numerical expressions used in our experiments are: 'more than a quarter', 'around 98.2%', 'just over 25 per cent' or 'less than 100 kilometres'.

4.2 Levels of difficulty

The Mathematics Curriculum of the Qualifications and Curriculum Authority (1999) describes a number of teaching levels and we assume that concepts to be taught at lower levels will be simpler than ones taught at higher levels. Following this idea a Scale of Mathematic Concepts is defined to identify the different levels of difficulty to understand mathematic concepts. The scale defined from less to greater difficulty is: numerical expression in numbers *(600)*, words *(six)*, fractions *(1/4)*, ratios *(1 in 4)*, percentages *(25%)* and decimal percentages *(33.8%)*.

From the Scale of Mathematic Concepts defined, different levels of difficulty are considered in our system. There are three different levels (from easiest to hardest):

1. *Fractions Level*: each percentage in the text is adapted using fractions as mathematical form for the quantity, and sometimes a hedge is used.
2. *Percentages without decimals Level (PWD)*: the system rounds the original percentage with decimals and uses hedges if they are needed.
3. *Percentages with decimals Level*: This is the most difficult level where no adaptation is performed.

The system operates only on numerical expressions at the highest levels of the scale (the most difficult levels), that is, numerical expression given in percentages or decimal percentages, adapting them to other levels of less difficulty. So, the user can select the level to which adapt the original numerical expression from the text. Using the interface of the system, the level of difficulty is chosen by the final user and the numerical expressions from the text with higher level of difficulty than the level chosen are adapted following the rules defined.

4.3 Set of strategies

A set of strategies is defined so they can be applied to adapt the original numerical expression. The quantity of the expression is replaced with another expression and sometimes numerical hedges are added to create the simplified numerical expression.

The use of hedges to simplify numerical expression can be influenced by three parameters. The first is the type of simplification depending on the mathematical knowledge of the final user. The second is the simplification strategy for the choice of the final mathematical form. And the last is the loss of precision that occurs when the expression is simplified.

Out of the European Guidelines for the Production of Easy-to-Read Information for People with Learning Disability (Freyhoff et al., 1998), only one involves the treatment of numbers: "Be careful with numbers. If you use small numbers, always use the number and not the word". For example, if the texts says 'four', the system adapts it by '4' following this European Guideline. This strategy is applied by the system at all levels.

There are other strategies to adapt numerical expressions in the form of percentage to other levels of difficulty: (1) replace decimal percentages with percentages without decimals; (2) replace decimal percentages with ratios; (3) replace percentages with ratios; (4) replace decimal percentages with fractions; (5) replace percentages with fractions; (6) replace ratios with fractions; (7) replace numerical expressions in words with numerical expressions in digits.

At each level of difficulty, a subset of the strategies is applied to simplify the numerical expression. For the *Fractions Level* the strategies 4, 5 and 7 are used. For the *Percentages with decimals Level* the strategies 1 and 7 are applied. And for the last level, *Percentages without decimals Level* only the last strategy, number 7, is used.

4.4 System operation

The system takes as input the original text. The user of the system has to choose the level of difficulty. A set of numerical expressions are selected and a set of transformations is applied to adapt them, generating as output of the system a text with the numerical expressions simplified at the chosen level.

The system works through several phases to adapt the numerical expressions in the input text. Some of them are internal working phases (2, 4 and 5). The rest of them (1, 3 and 6) are phases where the user of the system plays a role. The phases considered in the system are:

1. **Input text**: an original text is selected to adapt its numerical expressions.

2. **Mark Numerical Expressions**: the numerical expressions that can be adapted are marked.

3. **Choose the level of difficulty**: the user chooses the desired level of difficulty for the numerical expressions in the text.

4. **Adapt the numerical expression from the text**: each numerical expression is adapted if the level of the numerical expression is higher than the level of difficulty chosen.

5. **Replace numerical expression in the text**: adapted numerical expressions replace the originals in the text.

6. **Output text**: the final adapted version of the text is presented to the user.

The next subsections presents how the system acts in each phase and what kind of tools are used to achieve the final text.

4.4.1 Phase 1: Input text

In this first phase, a plain text is chosen as input to the system to adapt its numerical expressions. Using a Graphical User Interface (GUI) in Java, the user can upload an original text.

4.4.2 Phase 2: Mark numerical expressions

For the text chosen, the system executes the *Numerical Expression Parser*[1]. Using this parser the numerical quantities are annotated with their type (cardinal, fraction, percentage, decimal percentage, etc.), their format (words, digits), their value *(Vg)*, their units, and hedging phrases, such as 'more than'. The input to the program is the plain text file and the output is the text with sentences and numerical expressions annotated in XML format. In the following code we can see how a numerical quantity is annotated in the parser.

> Overall figures showed the national pass rate soared
> **<numex hedge="above" hedge-sem="greaterthan" type="percentage" format="digits" Vg="0.97">**
> above 97% **</numex>**

The XML file is treated by the system and numerical expressions are marked in the original text. So, the user can see which numerical expressions are going to be adapted by the system (in the next phase) depending on the level of difficulty chosen.

4.4.3 Phase 3: Choose the level of difficulty

The user of the system chooses the level of difficulty to adapt the original numerical expressions. There are three levels: *fractions*, *percentages without decimals* and *percentages with decimals*.

4.4.4 Phase 4: Adapt the Numerical Expressions

After deciding the level of difficulty, the system has to adapt each numerical expression to generate the final version. The process of simplification has two stages: obtaining the candidate and applying the adaptation and hedge choice rules.

From the XML file produced by the parser the following information for a numerical expression is obtained: (1) if there is or not hedge and the kind of hedge; (2) the type (cardinal, fraction, percentage, decimal percentage) and format (digits or words) of the original numerical expression; (3) the *given value (Vg)* translated from the original numerical expression value of the text; and (4) the units from the

[1]For more details see (Williams, 2010)

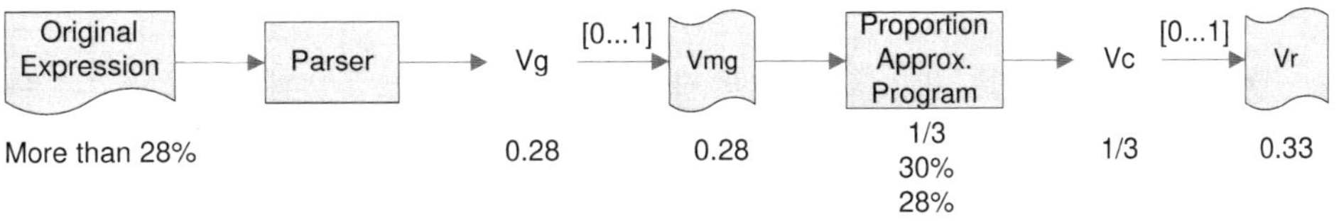

Figure 1: Obtaining the candidate for simplification. The original expression is annotated by the parser (Vg), and this value is normalized (Vmg). A candidate substitute value (Vc) is chosen from the *proportion approximation program* and normalized (Vr).

original expression (M, ins, grams). For example, if in the text the original numerical expression is a percentage like '25.9%', there is no hedge, the type is 'decimal percentage', the format is 'digits', *Vg* is 0.259 and there are no units. In the expression, '20 grams', there is no hedge, the type is 'cardinal', the format is 'digits', *Vg* is 20 and the parser annotates the units with 'g'.

The given value *Vg* annotated by the parser is transformed into a value between 0 to 1, referred to as *mapping given value (Vmg)*, which represents the proportion under consideration. This value is given as input to the *proportion approximation program* (Power and Williams, 2012), which returns a list of candidates for substitution. From this list, the first option is taken as *candidate substitute value (Vc)*, because the program returns them in decreasing order of precision. This means that the most precise candidate at the required level of difficulty is chosen. The program also might return the values "none" and "all" if the input value is close to 0 or 1, respectively. From the *Vc* we calculate the *rounded value (Vr)* corresponding to the normalization of the candidate value between 0 to 1. For example, if *Fraction level* is chosen, for the original expression "more than 28%" with *Vmg=0.28*, the system chooses *Vc*=1/3 with *Vr=0.33*. The whole process can be seen in Figure 1.

An additional level of adaptation is required beyond simple replacement with the candidate substitute value. If the original numerical expressions in the text are difficult to understand, the system must adapt them to the desired level of difficulty. For each numerical expression, the system only applies the adaptation rules if the difficulty level of the numerical expression is higher than the level of difficulty chosen by the user. This is captured by a set of three adaptation rules:

- If the type of the numerical expression is 'cardinal' and the format is 'words' then the candidate to be used in the simplification is *Vg*. For example, if the original numerical expression is 'six', it will be replaced by '6'.

- In a similar way, if the type is 'fraction' (the lowest possible level of difficulty) and the format is also 'words' then the candidate is obtained by applying the *proportion approximation program*. For example, if the original numerical expression is 'a quarter', it would be replaced by '1/4'.

- If the type is 'percentages' or 'decimal percentages' and the format is 'digits' then the candidate is calculated by the *proportion approximation program* provided that the level of difficulty chosen in the GUI was lower than the level of the calculated numerical expression.

In order to complete the simplification, the system has to decide if a hedge should be used to achieve the final version of the adapted numerical expression. This decision is taken based on the difference in value between the value of the original expression in the text *(Vg)* and the value of the candidate substitute *(Vc)* (as given by the relative difference between the normalized values *Vr* and *Vmg* calculated in the first stage). The actual hedge used in the original expression (if any) is also considered. The various possible combinations of these values, and the corresponding choice of final hedge, are described in Table 1, which presents all possible options to decide in each case, the hedge and the value corresponding to the final numerical expression. For example, if the original expression is "more than 28%", we have Vc=1/3, Vmg=0.28 and Vr=0.33. Then Vr>Vmg so the corresponding choice of the final hedge is in the

OriginalNumExp	if Vr>Vmg	if Vr=Vmg	if Vr<Vmg
more than OrigValue	around Vc	more than Vc	more than Vc
exactly OrigValue	less than Vc	exactly Vc	more than Vc
less than OrigValue	less than Vc	less than Vc	around Vc
OrigValue	around Vc	Vc	around Vc

Table 1: Hedge Choice Rules. For each original expression (OrigValue), the normalized values *(Vmg, Vr)* are used to determinate the hedge chosen for the simplified expression. The final version is composed by the hedge chosen and the candidate value *(Vc)*

first column of Table 1 ("around") and the simplified expression is "around 1/3".

When the user chooses the *Fraction Level* in the system, every numerical expression with difficulty level greater than fraction level will be replaced by a numerical expression expressed in fraction form. Depending on the values *Vr* and *Vmg*, the appropriate hedge will be chosen.

4.4.5 Phase 5: Replace numerical expressions

Once the system has applied its rules, an adapted version is available for each original numerical expression which was more difficult than the target difficulty level. The output text is obtained by replacing these difficult expressions with the corresponding simplified version.

5 Evaluation of the system

This section presents the evaluation of the system, describing the materials, experiment, participants and results of the evaluation.

5.1 Materials

We selected for the experiment a set of eight candidate sentences from the NUMGEN corpus, but the number of numerical expressions was larger as some sentences contained more than one proportion expression. In total we had 13 numerical expressions. We selected sentences with as many variations in context, precision and different wordings as possible. The range of proportions values was from points nearly 0.0 to almost 1.0, to give coverage to a wide spread of proportion values. We considered values in the central range (say 0.2 to 0.8) and values at the extreme ranges (say 0.0-0.2 and 0.8-1.0). We also classified as common values the well-known percentages and fractions like 25%, 50%, 1/4 and 1/2, and as uncommon values the rest like 15% or 6/7.

5.2 Experiment

To evaluate the system a questionnaire was presented to a set of human evaluators. The experiment was created and presented on SurveyMonkey[2], a commonly-used provider of web surveys. For each original sentence, we presented two possible simplifications generated by the system. Participants were asked to use their judgement to decide whether they agreed that the simplified sentences were acceptable for the original sentence. A Likert scale of four values (Strongly Disagree, Disagree, Agree, Strongly Agree) was used to collect the answers.

In the survey only two levels of adaptation from the original sentence were presented. The first option generated by the system was for the *Fractions level*. The second option generated by the system was for the *Percentages without decimals (PWD)*.

5.3 Participants

The task of simplifying numerical expressions is difficult, so we selected a group of 34 experts made up of primary or secondary school mathematics teachers or adult basic numeracy tutors, all native English speakers. This group is well qualified to tackle the task since they are highly numerate and accustomed to talking to people who do not understand mathematical concepts very well. We found participants through personal contacts and posts to Internet forums for mathematics teachers and numeracy tutors.

5.4 Results

The answers from the participants were evaluated. In total we collected 377 responses, 191 responses for the *Fraction level* and 186 responses for the *Percentage without decimals (PWD)*. Table 2 shows the average from the collected responses, considering 1

[2]http://www.surveymonkey.com/s/WJ69L86

Level	Total average	Values	Average	Values	Average
Fraction	2,44	Central	2,87	Common	2,59
		Extreme	2,14	Uncommon	1,21
PWD	2,96	Central	3,00	Common	2,80
		Extreme	2,96	Uncommon	3,22

Table 2: System Evaluation: Fraction Level and Percentages Without Decimals (PWD)

Opinion	Fraction Level	PWD Level
Strongly Disagree	19%	6%
Disagree	27%	15%
Agree	43%	56%
Strongly Agree	11%	23%

Table 3: Opinion of the experts in percentages

to 4 for strongly disagree to strongly agree. In addition, Table 3 shows the distribution in percentages of the opinion of the experts. At the *Fraction level*, there is not too much difference between the average of the answers of the experts that agree with the system and those that disagree. Most experts are neutral. But for the *PWD level* the average shows that most experts agree with the simplification done.

We have also analyzed the answers considering two different criteria from the original numerical expressions: when they are central (20% to 80%) or extreme values (0% to 20% and 80% to 100%), and when the original numerical expressions are common or uncommon values. In general terms, the experts think that the simplification done by the system in the *PWD level* is better than the simplification done in the *Fraction level*. They disagree specially with the simplification using fractions in two cases. One is the treatment of the extreme values where the system obtains as possible candidates "none" and "all"[3]. Another case is when uncommon fractions are used to simplify the numerical expression, like for example 9/10. In these two cases the average is lower than the rest of the average achieved.

5.5 Discussion

The system combines syntactic transformations (via the introduction of hedges) and lexical substitutions (by replacing actual values with substitution candidates and transforming quantities expressed as words into digits) to simplify the original numerical expression. These kinds of transformations are different from those used by other systems, which rely only on syntactic transformations or only on lexical substitutions. Rules are purpose-specific and focused on numerical expressions. With this kind of transformations the readability of the text improves in spite of the fact that the resulting syntactic structure of the numerical expression is more complicated, due to the possible presence of hedges. For example, for a original numerical expression like '25.9%' the system generates the simplified 'more than a quarter' which is easier to understand even though longer and syntactically more complex.

With respect to coverage of different types of numerical expressions, this system does not consider *ratios* as a possible simplification strategy because the *proportion approximation program* does not use them as candidates to simplify a proportion. This possibility should be explored in the future.

Another observation is that the system does not consider the context of the sentence in which the numerical expression occurs. For example, if the sentence makes a comparison between two numerical expressions that the system rounded to the same value, the original meaning is lost. One example of this case is the following sentence from the corpus: "One in four children were awarded A grades (25.9%, up from 25.3% last year)". Both percentages '25.9%' and '25.3%' are simplified by the system using 'around 1/4' and the meaning of the sentence is lost. Thus we should consider the role of context (the set of numerical expressions in a given sentence as a whole and the meaning of the text) in establishing what simplifications must be used.

[3] See (Power and Williams, 2012) for a discussion of appropriate hedges for values near the extreme points of 0 and 1.

6 Conforming with conclusions of prior surveys

The results presented for the system are evaluated in this section for conformance with the conclusions resulting from the empirical studies described in (Bautista et al., 2011b) and (Bautista et al., 2011a).

With respect to the preference for round or common values in simplification (Conclusion 1), the system presented conforms to this preference by virtue of the way in which the list of candidate substitutions is produced by the program. The candidates returned by the program are already restricted to common values of percentages (rounded up) and fractions, so the decision to consider as preferred candidate the one listed first implicitly applies the criteria that leads to this behavior.

With respect to the need to treat differently values in the extreme or central ranges of proportion (Conclusion 2), the system addresses this need by virtue of the actual set of candidates produced by the program in each case. For example, if the original expression is a extreme value like '0.972', the program produces a different candidate substitution ('almost all') that in the central ranges is not considered.

With respect to restricting the use of hedges to situations where loss of precision is incurred (Conclusion 3), the hedge choice rules applied by the system (see Table 1) satisfy this restriction. When $Vr{=}Vmg$ hedges are included in the simplified expression only if they were already present in the original expression.

In addition, the system rounds up any quantities with decimal positions to the nearest whole number whenever the decimal positions are lost during simplification. This functionality is provided implicitly by the program, which presents the rounded up version as the next option immediately following the alternative which includes the decimal positions. For example, if the input proportion is '0.198', some rounded candidate substitutions are calculated as 'almost 20%' or 'less than 20%'.

Finally, the system follows the European guidelines for the production of easy to read information in that it automatically replaces numerical quantities expressed in words with the corresponding quantity expressed in digits.

7 Conclusions and future work

The system described in this paper constitutes a first approximation to the task of simplifying numerical expressions in a text to varying degrees of difficulty. The definition of an scale of difficulty of numerical expressions, the identification of rules governing the selection of candidate substitution and the application of hedges constitute important contributions. The empirical evaluation of the system with human experts results in acceptable rates of agreement. The behavior of the system conforms to the conclusions on simplification strategies as applied by humans resulting from previous empirical surveys.

There are different aspects to improve the actual system from the data collected, with a special attention to cases in which the experts disagree. As future work, the syntactic context should be considered to simplify numerical expression, extending the kind of proportion to simplify and treating special cases analyzed in this first version. At the syntactic level, some transformation rules can be implemented from a syntactic analysis. It is important that the meaning of the sentences be preserved regardless of whether part of the sentence is deleted or rewritten by the adaptation rules. In addition, the numerical expression parser and the proportion approximation program could also be studied in order to evaluate the impact of their errors in the final performance.

Our final aim is to develop an automatic simplification system in a broader sense, possibly including more complex operations like syntactic transformations of the structure of the input text, or lexical substitution to reduce the complexity of the vocabulary employed in the text. Additionally we hope to develop versions of the simplification system for other languages, starting with Spanish. Probably the simplification strategies for numbers would be the same but the use of hedge modifiers may be different.

Acknowledgments

This research is funded by the Spanish Ministry of Education and Science (TIN2009-14659-C03-01 Project), Universidad Complutense de Madrid and Banco Santander Central Hispano (GR58/08 Research Group Grant), and the FPI grant program.

References

Susana Bautista, Pablo Gervás, and Ignacio Madrid. 2009. Feasibility Analysis for SemiAutomatic Conversion of Text to Improve Readability. In *Proceedings of The Second International Conference on Information and Communication Technologies and Accessibility*, Hammamet, Tunusia, May.

Susana Bautista, Raquel Hervás, Pablo Gervás, Richard Power, and Sandra Williams. 2011a. Experimental identification of the use of hedges in the simplification of numerical expressions. In *Proceedings of the Second Workshop on Speech and Language Processing for Assistive Technologies*, pages 128–136, Edinburgh, Scotland, UK, July. Association for Computational Linguistics.

Susana Bautista, Raquel Hervás, Pablo Gervás, Richard Power, and Sandra Williams. 2011b. How to Make Numerical Information Accessible: Experimental Identification of Simplification Strategies. In Campos, Pedro and Graham, Nicholas and Jorge, Joaquim and Nunes, Nuno and Palanque, Philippe and Winckler, Marco, editor, *Human-Computer Interaction INTERACT 2011*, volume 6946 of *Lecture Notes in Computer Science*, pages 57–64. Springer Berlin / Heidelberg.

Ann M. Bisantz, Stephanie Schinzing, and Jessica Munch. 2005. Displaying uncertainty: Investigating the effects of display format and specificity. *Human Factors: The Journal of the Human Factors and Ergonomics Society*, 47(4):777.

Yvonne Canning. 2000. Cohesive simplification of newspaper text for aphasic readers. In *3rd annual CLUK Doctoral Research Colloquium*.

Raman Chandrasekar and Bangalore Srinivas. 1997. Automatic induction of rules for text simplification. *Knowledge-Based Systems*, 10.

Raman Chandrasekar, Christine Doran, and Bangalore Srinivas. 1996. Motivations and methods for text simplification. In *In Proceedings of the Sixteenth International Conference on Computational Linguistics (COLING '96)*, pages 1041–1044.

Clark Christina and Douglas Jonathan. 2010. Young people reading and writing today: Whether, what and why. Technical report, London: National Literacy Trust.

Walter Daelemans, Anja Hothker, and Erik Tjong Kim Sang. 2004. Automatic Sentence Simplification for Subtitling in Dutch and English. In *Proceedings of the 4th Conference on Language Resources and Evaluation*, pages 1045–1048, Lisbon, Portugal.

Siobhan Devlin and John Tait. 1998. *The use of a Psycholinguistic database in the Simplification of Text for Aphasic Readers*. Lecture Notes. Stanford, USA: CSLI.

Nathan Dieckmann, Paul Slovic, and Ellen Peters. 2009. The use of narrative evidence and explicit likelihood by decision makers varying in numeracy. *Risk Analysis*, 29(10).

Geert Freyhoff, Gerhard Hess, Linda Kerr, Elizabeth Menzel, Bror Tronbacke, and Kathy Van Der Veken. 1998. European guidelines for the production of easy-to-read information.

Caroline Gasperin, Lucia Specia, Tiago F. Pereira, and Sandra M. Aluisio. 2009. Learning when to simplify sentences for natural text simplification. In *Proceedings of the Encontro Nacional de Inteligencia Artificial (ENIA)*, pages 809–818, Bento Gonalves, Brazil.

Deeqa Jama and George Dugdale. 2010. Literacy: State of the nation. Technical report, National Literacy Trust.

Arnaldo Candido Jr., Erick Maziero, Caroline Gasperin, Thiago A. S. Pardo, Lucia Specia, and Sandra M. Aluisio. 2009. Supporting the Adaptation of Texts for Poor Literacy Readers: a Text Simplification Editor for Brazilian Portuguese. In *Proceedings of the NAACL/HLT Workshop on Innovative Use of NLP for Building Educational Applications*, pages 34–42, Boulder, Colorado.

Imtiaz Hussain Khan, Kees Deemter, and Graeme Ritchie. 2008. Generation of refering expressions: managing structural ambiguities. In *Proceedings of the 22nd International Conference on Computational Linguistics(COLING)*, pages 433–440, Manchester.

Himanshu Mishra, Arul Mishra, and Baba Shiv. 2011. In praise of vagueness: malleability of vague information as a performance booster. *Psychological Science*, 22(6):733–8, April.

Ellen Peters, Judith Hibbard, Paul Slovic, and Nathan Dieckmann. 2007. Numeracy skill and the communication, comprehension, and use of risk-benefit information. *Health Affairs*, 26(3):741–748.

Sarah E. Petersen and Mari Ostendorf. 2007. Text Simplification for Language Learners: A Corpus Analysis. In *Proceedings of Workshop on Speech and Language Technology for Education (SLaTE)*.

Richard Power and Sandra Williams. 2012. Generating numerical approximations. *Computational Linguistics*, 38(1).

Qualification and Curriculum Authority. 1999. Mathematics: the National Curriculum for England. Department for Education and Employment, London.

Advaith Siddharthan. 2002. Resolving attachment and clause boundary amgiguities for simplifying relative clause constructs. In *Proceedings of the Student Research Workshop, 40th Meeting of the Association for Computacional Linguistics*.

Advaith Siddharthan. 2003. *Syntactic Simplification and Text Cohesion*. Ph.D. thesis, University of Cambridge.

United Nations. 1994. Standard Rules on the Equalization of Opportunities for Persons with Disabilities. Technical report.

Sandra Williams and Richard Power. 2009. Precision and mathematical form in first and subsequent mentions of numerical facts and their relation to document structure. In *Proc. of the 12th European Workshop on Natural Language Generation*, Athens.

Sandra Williams and Ehud Reiter. 2005. Generating readable texts for readers with low basic skills. In *Proceeding of the 10th European Workshop on Natural Language Generation*, pages 140–147, Aberdeen, Scotland.

Joel Williams, Sam Clemens, Karin Oleinikova, and Karen Tarvin. 2003a. The Skills for Life survey: A national needs and impact survey of literacy, numeracy and ICT skills. Technical Report Research Report 490, Department for Education and Skills.

Sandra Williams, Ehud Reiter, and Liesl Osman. 2003b. Experiments with discourse-level choices and readability. In *In Proceedings of the European Natural Language Generation Workshop (ENLG) and 11th Conference of the European Chapter of the Association for Computational Linguistics (EACL03)*, pages 127–134.

Sandra Williams. 2010. A Parser and Information Extraction System for English Numerical Expressions. Technical report, The Open University, Milton Keynes, MK7 6AA, U.K.

A Two-Stage Approach for Generating Unbiased Estimates of Text Complexity

Kathleen M. Sheehan **Michael Flor** **Diane Napolitano**

Educational Testing Service
Princeton, NJ, USA
{ksheehan, mflor, dnapolitano}@ets.org

Abstract

Many existing approaches for measuring text complexity tend to overestimate the complexity levels of informational texts while simultaneously underestimating the complexity levels of literary texts. We present a two-stage estimation technique that successfully addresses this problem. At Stage 1, each text is classified into one or another of three possible genres: informational, literary or mixed. Next, at Stage 2, a complexity score is generated for each text by applying one or another of three possible prediction models: one optimized for application to informational texts, one optimized for application to literary texts, and one optimized for application to mixed texts. Each model combines lexical, syntactic and discourse features, as appropriate, to best replicate human complexity judgments. We demonstrate that resulting text complexity predictions are both unbiased, and highly correlated with classifications provided by experienced educators.

1 Introduction

Automated text analysis systems, such as readability metrics, are frequently used to assess the probability that texts with varying combinations of linguistic features will be more or less accessible to readers with varying levels of reading comprehension skill (Stajner, Evans, Orasan and Mitkov, 2012). This paper introduces TextEvaluator, a fully-automated text analysis system designed to facilitate such work.[1] TextEvaluator successfully addresses an important limitation of many existing readability metrics: the tendency to over-predict the complexity levels of informational texts, while simultaneously under-predicting the complexity levels of literary texts (Sheehan, Kostin & Futagi, 2008; Sheehan, Kostin, Futagi & Flor, 2010). We illustrate this phenomenon, and argue that it results from two fundamental differences between informational and literary texts: (a) differences in the way that common every-day words are used and combined; and (b) differences in the rate at which rare words are repeated.

Our approach for addressing these differences can be summarized as follows. First, a large set of lexical, syntactic and discourse features is extracted from each text. Next, either human raters, or an automated genre classifier is used to classify each text into one or another of three possible genre categories: informational, literary, or mixed. Finally, a complexity score is generated for each text by applying one or another of three possible prediction models: one optimized for application to informational texts, one optimized for application to literary texts, and one optimized for application to mixed texts. We demonstrate that resulting complexity measures are both unbiased, and highly correlated with text grade level (GL) classifications provided by experienced educators.

[1] TextEvaluator was previously called SourceRater.

Our paper is organized as follows. Section 2 summarizes related work on readability assessment. Section 3 describes the two corpora assembled for use in this study, and outlines how genre and GL classifications were assigned. Section 4 illustrates the problem of genre bias by considering the specific biases detected in two widely-used readability metrics. Section 5 describes the TextEvaluator features, methods and results. Section 6 presents a summary and discussion.

2 Related Work

Despite the large numbers of text features that may potentially contribute to the ease or difficulty of comprehending complex text, many widely-used readability metrics are based on extremely limited feature sets. For example, the Flesch-Kincaid GL score (Kincaid, et al., 1975), the FOG Index (Gunning, 1952), and the Lexile Framework (Stenner, et al., 2006) each consider just two features: a single measure of syntactic complexity (average sentence length) and a single measure of lexical difficulty (either average word length in syllables, average frequency of multi-syllable words, or average word familiarity estimated via a word frequency, WF, index).

Recently, more computationally sophisticated modeling techniques such as Statistical Language Models (Si and Callan, 2001; Collins-Thompson and Callan, 2004, Heilman, et al., 2007, Pitler and Nenkova, 2008), Support Vector Machines (Schwarm and Ostendorf, 2005), Principal Components Analyses (Sheehan, et al., 2010) and Multi-Layer Perceptron classifiers (Vajjala and Meurers, 2012) have enabled researchers to investigate a broader range of potentially useful features. For example: Schwarm and Ostendorf (2005) demonstrated that vocabulary measures based on trigrams were effective at distinguishing articles targeted at younger and older readers; Pitler and Nenkova (2008) reported improved validity for measures based on the likelihood of vocabulary and the likelihood of discourse relations; and Vajjala and Meurers (2012) demonstrated that features inspired by Second Language Acquisition research also contributed to validity improvements. Importantly, however, while this research has contributed to our understanding of the types of text features that may cause texts to be more or less comprehensible, evaluations focused on the presence and degree of genre bias have not been reported.

3 Corpora

Two text collections are considered in this research. Our training corpus includes 934 passages selected from a set of previously administered standardized assessments constructed to provide valid and reliable feedback about the types of verbal reasoning skills described in U.S. state and national assessment frameworks. Human judgments of genre (informational, literary or mixed) and GL (grades 3-12) were available for all texts. Genre classifications were based on established guidelines which place texts structured to inform or persuade (e.g., newspaper text, excerpts from science or social studies textbooks) in the informational category, and texts structured to provide a rewarding literary experience (e.g., folk tales, short stories, excerpts from novels) in the literary category (see American Institutes for Research, 2008). We added a Mixed category to accommodate texts classified as incorporating both informational and literary elements. Nelson, Perfetti, Liben and Liben (2012) describe an earlier, somewhat smaller version of this dataset. We added additional passages downloaded from State Department of Education web sites, and from the National Assessment of Educational Progress (NAEP). In each case, GL classifications reflected the GLs at which passages were administered to students. Thus, all passages classified at Grade 3 appeared on high-stakes assessments constructed to provide evidence of student performance relative to Grade 3 reading standards.

Two important characteristics of this dataset should be noted. First, unlike many previous corpora, (e.g., Stenner, et al., 2006; Zeno, et al., 2005) accurate paragraph markings are included for all texts. Second, while many of the datasets considered in previous readability research were comprised entirely of informational text (e.g., Pitler and Nenkova, 2008; Schwarm and Ostendorf, 2005; Vajjala and Meurers, 2012) the current dataset covers the full range of text types considered by teachers and students in U.S. classrooms.

Table 1 shows the numbers of informational, literary and mixed training passages at each targeted GL. Passage lengths ranged from 112 words at Grade 3, to more than 2000 words at Grade 12.

Average passage lengths were 569 words and 695 words in the informational and literary subsets, respectively.

Grade	Genre			
Level	Inf.	Lit.	Mixed	Total
3	46	60	8	114
4	51	74	7	132
5	44	46	12	102
6	41	40	6	87
7	36	58	6	100
8	70	63	18	151
9	23	23	2	48
10	26	49	2	77
11	15	24	0	39
12	47	15	22	84
Total	399	452	83	934

Table 1. Numbers of passages in the model development/training dataset, by grade level and genre.

A validation dataset was also constructed. It includes the 168 texts that were published as Appendix B of the new Common Core State Standards (CCSSI, 2010), a new standards document that has now been adopted in 46 U.S. states. Individual texts were contributed by teachers, librarians, curriculum experts, and reading researchers. GL classifications are designed to illustrate the "staircase of increasing complexity" that teachers and test developers are being encouraged to replicate when selecting texts for use in K-12 instruction and assessment in the U.S. The staircase is specified in terms of five grade bands: Grades 2-3, Grades 4-5, Grades 6-8, Grades 9-10 or Grades 11+. Table 2 shows the numbers of informational, literary and "Other" texts (includes both Mixed and speeches) included at each grade band.

Grade	Genre			
Band	Inf.	Lit.	Other	Total
2-3	6	10	4	20
4-5	16	10	4	30
6-8	12	16	13	41
9-10	12	10	17	39
11+	8	10	20	38
Total	54	56	58	168

Table 2. Numbers of passages in the validation dataset, by grade band and genre.

4 Genre Bias

This section examines the root causes of genre bias. We focus on two fundamental differences between informational and literary texts: differences in the types of vocabularies employed, and differences in the rate at which rare words are repeated. These differences have been examined in several previous studies. For example, Lee (2001) documented differences in the use of "core" vocabulary within a corpus of informational and literary texts that included over one million words downloaded from the British National Corpus. Core vocabulary was defined in terms of a list of 2000 common words classified as appropriate for use in the dictionary definitions presented in the Longman Dictionary of Contemporary English. The analyses demonstrated that core vocabulary usage was higher in literary texts than in informational texts. For example, when literary texts such as fiction, poetry and drama were considered, the percent of total words classified as "core" vocabulary ranged from 81% to 84%. By contrast, when informational texts such as science and social studies texts were considered, the percent of total words classified as "core" vocabulary ranged from 66% to 71%. In interpreting these results Lee suggested that the creativity and imaginativeness typically associated with literary writing may be less closely tied to the type or level of vocabulary employed and more closely tied to the way that core words are used and combined. Note that this implies that an individual word detected in a literary text may not be indicative of the same level of processing challenge as that same word detected in an informational text.

Differences in the vocabularies employed within informational and literary texts, and subsequent impacts on readability metrics, are also discussed in Appendix A of the Common Core State Standards (CCSSI, 2010). The tendency of many existing readability metrics to underestimate the complexity levels of literary texts is described as follows: "The Lexile Framework, like traditional formulas, may underestimate the difficulty of texts that use simple, familiar language to convey sophisticated ideas, as is true of much high-quality fiction written for adults and appropriate for older students" (p. 7).

Genre bias may also result from genre-specific differences in word repetition rates. Hiebert and

Mesmer (2013, p.46) describe this phenomenon as follows: "Content area texts often receive inflated readability scores since key concept words that are rare (e.g., *photosynthesis*, *inflation*) are often repeated which increases vocabulary load, even though repetition of content words can support student learning (Cohen & Steinberg, 1983)".

Table 3 provides empirical evidence of these trends. The table presents mean GL classifications estimated conditional on mean WF scores, for the informational (n = 399) and literary (n = 452) passages in our training dataset. WF scores were generated via an in-house WF index constructed from a corpus of more than 400 million word tokens. The corpus includes more than 17,000 complete books, including both fiction and nonfiction titles.

	Informational			Literary		
Avg. WF	N	GL	SD	N	GL	SD
51.0–52.5	2	12.0	0.0	0	--	--
52.5–54.0	16	10.8	1.9	0	--	--
54.0–55.5	68	9.6	2.0	1	10.0	--
55.5–57.0	89	7.8	2.7	18	9.9	1.9
57.0–58.5	96	6.6	2.3	46	9.2	2.0
58.5–60.0	78	5.3	1.8	92	7.6	2.4
60.0–61.5	44	4.6	1.8	142	6.2	2.4
61.5–63.0	6	3.7	0.8	119	5.5	2.1
63.0–64.5	0	--	--	31	4.5	1.9
64.5–66.0	0	--	--	3	4.0	1.7
Total	399	57.4	2.1	452	60.6	1.9

Table 3. Mean GL classifications, by Average WF score, for informational and literary passages targeted at readers in grades 3 through 12.

The results in Table 3 confirm that, consistent with expectations, texts with lower average WF scores are more likely to appear on assessments targeted at older readers, while texts with higher average WF scores are more likely to appear on assessments targeted at younger readers. But note that large genre differences are also present. Figure 1 provides a graphical representation of these trends. Results for informational texts are plotted with a solid line; those for literary texts are plotted with a dashed line. Note that the literary curve appears above the informational curve throughout the entire observed range of the data. This suggests that a given value of the Average WF measure is indicative of a *higher* GL classification if the text in question is a literary text, and a *lower* GL classification if the text in question is an informational text. Since a readability measure that includes this feature (or a feature similar to this feature) without also accounting for genre effects will tend to yield predictions that fall *between* the two curves, resulting GL predictions will tend to be too high for informational texts (positive bias) and too low for literary texts (negative bias).

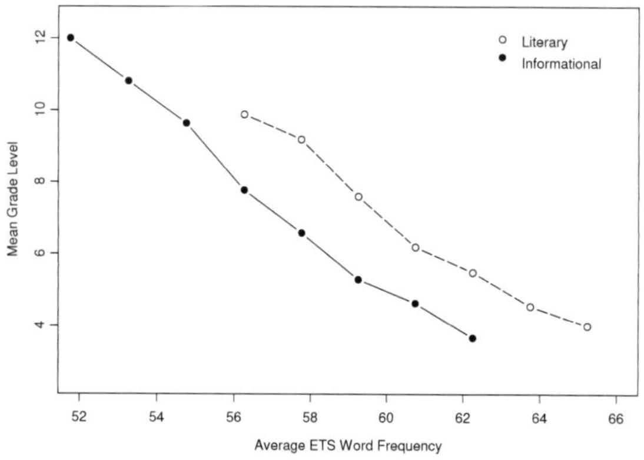

Figure 1. Mean text GL plotted conditional on average WF score. (One literary mean score based on evidence from a single text is not plotted.)

Figure 2 confirms that this evidence-based prediction holds true for two widely-used readability metrics: the Flesch-Kincaid GL score and the Lexile Framework[2]. Each individual plot compares Flesch-Kincaid GL scores (top row), or Lexile scores (bottom row) to the human GL classifications stored in our training dataset, i.e., classifications that were developed and reviewed by experienced educators, and were subsequently used to make high-stakes decisions about students and teachers, e.g., requiring students to repeat a grade rather than advancing to the next GL. The plots confirm that, in each case, the predicted pattern of over- and under-estimation is present. That is, on average, both Flesch-Kincaid scores and Lexile scores tend to be slightly too high for informational texts, and slightly too low for literary texts, thereby calling into doubt any cross-genre comparisons.

[2] All Lexile scores were obtained via the Lexile Analyzer available at www.lexile.com. Scores are only available for a subset of texts since our training corpus included just 548 passages at the time that these data were collected. Corresponding human GL classifications were approximately evenly distributed across grades 3 through 12.

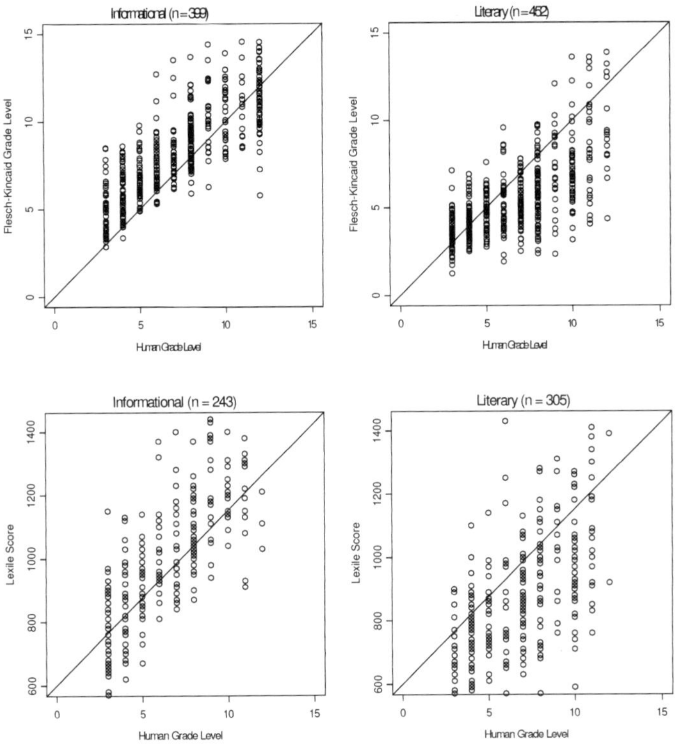

Figure 2. Passage complexity scores generated via the Flesch-Kincaid GL score (top) and the Lexile Framework (bottom) compared to GL classifications provided by experienced educators.

5 Features, Components and Results

5.1 Features

The TextEvaluator feature set is designed to measure the ease or difficulty of implementing four types of processes believed to be critically involved in comprehending complex text: (1) processes involved in word recognition and decoding, (2) processes associated with using relevant syntactic knowledge to assemble words into meaningful propositions, (3) processes associated with inferring connections across propositions or larger sections of text, and (4) processes associated with using relevant prior knowledge and experience to develop a more complete, more integrated mental representation of a text. (See Kintsch, 1998).

A total of 43 candidate features were developed. Since many of these were expected to be moderately inter-correlated, a Principal Components Analysis (PCA) was used to locate clusters of features that exhibited high within-cluster correlation and low between-cluster correlation. Linear combinations defined in terms of the resulting feature clusters provided the independent variables considered in subsequent investigations. Biber and his colleagues (2004) justify this approach by noting that, because many important aspects of text variation are not well captured by individual linguistic features, investigation of such characteristics requires a focus on "constellations of co-occurring linguistic features" as opposed to individual features (p. 45).

The PCA suggested that more than 60% of the variation captured by the full set of 43 features could be accounted for via a set of eight component scores, where each component is estimated as a linear combination of multiple correlated features, and only 3 of the 43 features had moderately high loadings on more than one component, and most loadings exceeded 0.70. The individual features comprising each component are described below.

Component #1: Academic Vocabulary. Ten features loaded heavily on this component. Two are based on the *Academic Word List* described in Coxhead (2000). These include: the frequency per thousand words of all words on the Academic Word List, and the ratio of listed words to total words. In a previous study, Vajjala and Meurers (2012) demonstrated that the ratio of listed words to total wards was very effective at distinguishing texts at lower and higher levels in the Weekly Reader corpus. Two additional features focus on the frequency of nominalizations, including one estimated from token counts and one estimated from type counts. Four additional features are based on word lists developed by Biber and his colleagues. These include the frequency per thousand words of academic verbs, abstract nouns, topical adjectives and cognitive process nouns (see Biber, 1986, 1988; and Biber, et al., 2004). Two measures of word length also loaded on this dimension: average word length measured in syllables, and the frequency per thousand words of words containing more than 8 characters.

Component #2: Syntactic Complexity. Seven features loaded heavily on this component. These include features determined from the output of the Stanford Parser (Klein and Manning, 2003), as well as more easily computed measures such as average sentence length, average frequency of long sentences (>= 25 words), and average number of words between punctuation marks (commas, semicolons, etc.). Parse-based features include average number of dependent clauses, and an automated version of the word "depth" measure introduced by Yngve (1960). This last feature, called Average Maximum Yngve Depth, is designed to capture variation in the memory load imposed by sentences with varying syntactic structures. It is estimated by first assigning a depth classification to each word in the text, then determining the maximum depth represented within each sentence, and then averaging over resulting sentence-level estimates to obtain a passage-level estimate. Several studies of this word depth measure have been reported. For example, Bormuth (1964) reported a correlation of -0.78 between mean word depth scores and cloze fill-in rates provided by Japanese EFL learners.

Component #3: Concreteness. Words that are more concrete are more likely to evoke meaningful mental images, a response that has been shown to facilitate comprehension (Coltheart, 1981). Alderson (2000) argued that the level of concreteness present in a text is a useful feature to consider when evaluating passages for use on reading assessments targeted at L2 readers. A total of five concreteness and imageability measures loaded heavily on this dimension. All five measures are based on concreteness and imageability ratings downloaded from the MRC psycholinguistic database (Coltheart, 1981). Ratings are expressed on a 7 point scale with 1 indicating least concrete, or least imageable, and 7 indicating most concrete or most imageable.

Component #4: Word Unfamiliarity. This component summarizes variation detected via six different features. Two features are measures of average word familiarity: one estimated via our inhouse WF Index, and one estimated via the TASA WF Index (see Zeno, et al., 1995). Both features have negative loadings, suggesting that the component is measuring vocabulary difficulty as opposed to vocabulary easiness. The other features with high loadings on this component are all measures of rare word frequency. These all have positive loadings since texts with large numbers of rare words are expected to be more difficult. Two types of rare word indices are included: indices based on token counts and indices based on type counts. Vocabulary measures based on token counts view each new word as an independent comprehension challenge, even when the same word occurs repeatedly throughout the text. By contrast, vocabulary measures based on type counts assume that a passage containing five different unfamiliar words may be more challenging than a passage containing the same unfamiliar word repeated five times. This difference is consistent with the notion that each repetition of an unknown word provides an additional opportunity to connect to prior knowledge (Cohen & Steinberg, 1983).

Component #5: Interactive/Conversational Style. This component includes the frequency per thousand words of: conversation verbs, fiction verbs, communication verbs, 1st person plural pronouns, contractions, and words enclosed in quotes. Verb types were determined from one or more of the following studies: Biber (1986), Biber (1988), and Biber, et al. (2004).

Component #6: Degree of Narrativity. Three features had high positive loadings on this dimension: Frequency of past perfect aspect verbs, frequency of past tense verbs and frequency of 3rd person singular pronouns. All three features have previously been classified as providing positive evidence of the degree of narrativity exhibited in a text (see Biber, 1986 and Biber, 1988).

Component #7: Cohesion. Cohesion is that property of a text that enables it to be interpreted as a "coherent message" rather than a collection of unrelated clauses and sentences. Halliday and Hasan (1976) argued that readers are more likely to interpret a text as a "coherent message" when certain observable features are present. These include repeated content words and explicit connectives. The seventh component extracted in the PCA includes three different types of cohesion features. The first two features measure the frequency of content word repetition across adjacent sentences within paragraphs. These measures differ from the cohesion measures discussed in Graesser et al. (2004) and in Pitler and Nenkova (2008) in that a psychometric linking procedure is used to ensure that results for different texts are reported on comparable scales (See Sheehan, in press). The frequency of causal conjuncts (*therefore*, *consequently*, etc.) also loads on this dimension.

Component #8: Argumentation. Two features have high loadings on this dimension: the frequency of concessive and adversative conjuncts (*although*, *though*, *alternatively*, *in contrast*, etc.), and the frequency of negations (*no*, *neither*, etc.), Just and Carpenter, (1987).

5.2 An Automated Genre Classifier

A preliminary automated genre classifier was developed by training a logistic regression model to predict the probability that a text is classified as *informational* as opposed to *literary*. A significant positive coefficient was obtained for the Academic Vocabulary component defined above, suggesting that a high score on this component may be interpreted as an indication that the text is more likely to be informational. Significant negative coefficients were obtained for Narrativity, Interactive/Conversational Style, and Syntactic Complexity, indicating that a high score on any of these components may be interpreted as an indication that the text is more likely to be literary. Two individual features that were not included in the PCA were also significant: the proportion of adjacent sentences containing at least one overlapping stemmed content word, and the frequency of 1st person singular pronouns. These features were not included in the PCA because they are not reliably indicative of differences in text complexity (See Sheehan, in press; Pitler and Nenkova, 2008.) Results confirmed, however, that these features are useful for predicting a text's genre classification.

Alternative decision rules based on this model were investigated. Table 4 summarizes the levels of precision (P), recall (R) and F1 = 2RP/(R+P) obtained for the selected decision rule which was defined as follows: Classify as informational if P(Inf) >= 0.52, classify as literary if P(inf) < 0.48, else classify as mixed. This decision rule is defined such that few texts are classified into the mixed category since, at present, the training dataset includes very few mixed texts. The table shows decreased precision in the Validation dataset since many more mixed texts are included, and the majority of these were classified as informational.

Dataset	Genre	N	R	P	F1
Training	Inf	399	.84	.79	.81
Training	Lit	452	.88	.79	.83
Training	Mixed	83	.01	.09	.01
Validation	Inf	67	.91	.56	.69
Validation	Lit	56	.80	.80	.80
Validation	Mixed	45	.07	1.0	.13

Table 4. Levels of Precision, Recall and F1 obtained for 1, 089 texts in the training and validation datasets. Speeches are not included in this summary.

5.3 Prediction Equations

We use separate genre-specific regression models to generate GL predictions for texts classified as informational, literary, or mixed. The coefficients estimated for informational and literary texts are shown in Table 5. Note that each component is significant in one or both models. The table also highlights key genre differences. For example, note that the Interactive/Conv. Style score is significant in the Inf. model but not in the Literary model. This reflects the fact that, while literary texts at all GLs tend to exhibit relatively high interactivity, similarly high interactivity among inf. texts tends to only be present at the lowest GLs. Thus, a high Interactivity is an indication of low complexity if the text in question is an informational text, but provides no statistically significant evidence about complexity if the text in question is a literary text.

Component	Informational	Literary
Academic Voc.	1.126*	.824*
Word Unfamiliarity	.802*	.793*
Word Concreteness	-.610*	-.483*
Syn. Complexity	.983*	1.404*
Lexical Cohesion	-.266*	-.440*
Interactive/Conv. Style	-.518*	*ns*
Degree of Narrativity	*ns*	-.361*
Argumentation	.431*	*ns*

Table 5. Regression coefficients estimated from training texts. $*p < .01$, *ns* = not significant.

5.4 Validity Evidence

Two aspects of system validity are of interest: (a) whether genre bias is present, and (b) whether complexity scores correlate well with judgments provided by professional educators, i.e., the educators involved in selecting texts for use on high-stakes state reading assessments. The issue of genre bias is addressed in Figure 3. Each plot compares GL predictions generated via TextEvaluator to GL predictions provided by experienced educators. Note that no evidence of a systematic tendency to under-predict the complexity levels of literary texts is present. This suggests that our strategy of developing distinct prediction models for informational and literary texts has succeeded in overcoming the genre biases present among many key features.

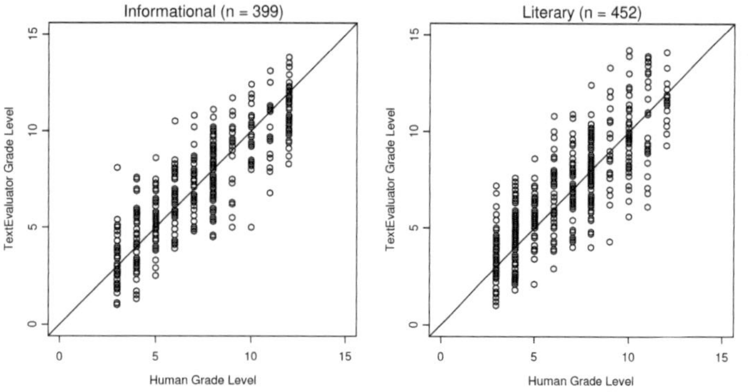

Figure 3. TextEvaluator GL predictions compared to human GL classifications for informational and literary texts.

TestEvaluator performance relative to the goal of predicting the human grade band classifications in the validation dataset was also examined. Results are summarized in Table 6 along with corresponding results for the Lexile Framework (Stenner, et al., 2006) and the REAP system (Heilman, et al., 2007). All results are reprinted, with permission, from Nelson, et al., (2012). In each case, performance is summarized in terms of the Spearman rank order correlation between the readability scores generated for each text, and corresponding human grade band classifications. 95% confidence limits estimated via the Fisher *r* to *z* transformation are also listed.

System	Lower 95% Bound	Correlation Coefficient	Upper 95% Bound
TextEvaluator	0.683	0.76	0.814
REAP	0.427	0.54	0.641
Lexile	0.380	0.50	0.607

Table 6. Correlation between readability scores and human grade band classifications for the 168 Common Core texts in the validation dataset.

The comparison suggests that, relative to the task of predicting the human grade band classifications assigned to the informational, literary and mixed texts in Appendix B of the new Common Core State Standards, TextEvaluator is significantly more effective than both the Lexile Framework and the REAP system.

6 Summary and Discussion

In many recent studies, proposed readability metrics have been trained and validated on text collections composed entirely of informational text, e.g., Wall Street Journal articles (Pitler and Nenkova, 2008), Encyclopedia Britannica articles (Schwarm and Ostendorf, 2005) and Weekly Reader articles (Vajjala and Meurers, 2012). This paper considers the more challenging task of predicting human-assigned GL classifications in a corpus of texts constructed to be representative of the broad range of reading materials considered by teachers and students in U.S. classrooms.

Two approaches for modeling the complexity characteristics of these passages were compared. In Approach #1, a single, non-genre specific prediction equation is estimated, and that equation is then applied to texts in all genres. Two measures developed via this approach were evaluated: the Lexile Framework and the REAP system.

Approach #2 differs from Approach #1 in that genre-specific prediction equations are used, thereby ensuring that important genre effects are accommodated. This approach is currently only available via the TextEvaluator system.

Measures developed via each approach were evaluated on a held-out sample. Results confirmed that complexity classifications obtained via TextEvaluator are significantly more highly correlated with the human grade band classifications in the held-out sample than are classifications obtained via the Lexile Framework or REAP system.

This study also demonstrated that, when genre effects are ignored, readability scores for informational texts tend to be overestimated, while those for literary texts tend to be underestimated. Note that this finding significantly complicates the process of using readability metrics to generate valid cross-genre comparisons. For example, Stajner, et al. (2012) conclude that SimpleWiki may not serve as a "gold standard" of high accessibility because comparisons based on readability metrics suggest that it is more complex than Fiction. We intend to further investigate this finding using TextEvaluator since conclusions that are not impacted by genre bias can then be reported. Additional planned work involves investigating additional measures of genre, and incorporating these into our genre classifier.

References

Alderson, J. C. (2000). *Assessing reading*. Cambridge: Cambridge University Press.

American Institutes for Research (2008). *Reading framework for the 2009 National Assessment of Educational Progress.* Washington, DC: National Assessment Governing Board.

Biber, D. (1986). Spoken and written textual dimension in English: Resolving the contradictory findings. *Language, 62*: 394-414.

Biber, D. (1988). *Variation across Speech and Writing.* Cambridge: Cambridge University Press.

Biber, D., Conrad, S., Reppen, R., Byrd, P., Helt, M., Clark, V., et al., (2004). *Representing language use in the university: Analysis of the TOEFL 2000 Spoken and Written Academic Language Corpus.* TOEFL Monograph Series, MS-25, January 2004. Princeton, NJ: Educational Testing Service.

Bormuth, J.R. (1964). Mean word depth as a predictor of comprehension difficulty. California *Journal of Educational Research, 15*, 226-231.

Cohen, S. A. & Steinberg, J. E. (1983). Effects of three types of vocabulary on readability of intermediate grade science textbooks: An application of Finn's transfer feature theory. *Reading Research Quarterly, 19*(1), 86-101.

Collins-Thompson, K. and Callan, J. (2004). A language modeling approach to predicting reading difficulty. In *Proceedings of HLT/NAACL 2004*, Boston, USA.

Coltheart, M. (1981). The MRC psycholinguistic database, *Quarterly Journal of Experimental Psychology, 33A*, 497-505.

Common Core State Standards Initiative (2010). *Common core state standards for English language arts & literacy in history/social studies, science and technical subjects.* Washington, DC: CCSSO & National Governors Association.

Coxhead, A. (2000) A new academic word list. *TESOL Quarterly, 34(2)*, 213-238.

Gunning, R. (1952). *The technique of clear writing*. McGraw-Hill: New York.

Graesser, A.C., McNamara, D. S., Louwerse, M.W. and Cai, Z. (2004). Coh-Metrix: Analysis of text on cohesion and language. *Behavior Research Methods, Instruments & Computers, 36*(2), 193-202.

Halliday, M. A.K. & Hasan, R. (1976) *Cohesion in English*. Longman, London.

Hiebert, E. H. & Mesmer, H. A. E. (2013). Upping the ante of text complexity in the Common Core State Standards: Examining its potential impact on young readers. *Educational Researcher, 42*(1), 44-51.

Heilman, M., Collins-Thompson, K., Callan, J. & Eskenazi, M. (2007). Combining lexical and grammatical features to improve readability measures for first and second language texts. In *Human Language Technologies 2007: The Conference of the North American Chapter of the Association for Computational Linguistics (HLT-NAACL'07)*, 460-467.

Just, M. A. & Carpenter, P. A. (1987). *The psychology of reading and language comprehension*. Boston: Allyn & Bacon.

Kincaid, J.P., Fishburne, R.P, Rogers, R.L. & Chissom, B.S. (1975). Derivation of new readability formulas (automated readability index, Fog count and Flesch reading ease formula) for navy enlisted personnel. Research Branch Report 8-75. Naval Air Station, Memphis, TN.

Kintsch, W. (1998). Comprehension: A paradigm for cognition. Cambridge, UK: Cambridge University Press.

Klein, D. & Manning, C. D. (2003). Accurate Unlexicalized Parsing. In *Proceedings of the 41st Meeting of the Association for Computational Linguistics*, 423-430.

Lee, D. Y. W. (2001) Defining core vocabulary and tracking its distribution across spoken and written genres. *Journal of English Linguistics. 29*, 250-278.

Nelson, J., Perfetti, C., Liben, D. and Liben, M. (2012). *Measures of text difficulty: Testing their predictive value for grade levels and student performance*. Technical Report, The Council of Chief State School Officers.

Pitler, E. & Nenkova, A (2008). Revisiting readability: A unified framework for predicting text quality. In *Proceedings of the 2008 Conference on Empirical Methods in Natural Language Processing,* Association for Computational Linguistics, 186-195.

Schwarm, S. & Ostendorf, M. (2005). Reading level assessment using support vector machines and statistical language models. In *Proceedings of the 43rd Annual Meeting of the Association for Computational Linguistics* (ACL'05), 523-530.

Sheehan, K.M. (in press). Measuring cohesion: An approach that accounts for differences in the degree of integration challenge presented by different types of sentences. *Educational Measurement: Issues and Practice.*

Sheehan, K.M., Kostin, I & Futagi, Y. (2008). When do standard approaches for measuring vocabulary difficulty, syntactic complexity and referential cohesion yield biased estimates of text difficulty? In B.C. Love, K. McRae, & V.M. Sloutsky (Eds.), *Proceedings of the 30th Annual Conference of the Cognitive Science Society*, Washington D.C.

Sheehan, K.M., Kostin, I., Futagi, Y. & Flor, M. (2010). *Generating automated text complexity classifications that are aligned with targeted text complexity standards.* (ETS RR-10-28). Princeton, NJ: ETS.

Si, L. & Callan, J. (2001). A statistical model for scientific readability. In *Proceedings of the 10th International Conference on Information and Knowledge Management (CIKM),* 574-576.

Štajner, S., Evans, R., Orasan, C., & Mitkov, R. (2012). What Can Readability Measures Really Tell Us About Text Complexity?. In *Natural Language Processing for Improving Textual Accessibility (NLP4ITA) Workshop Programme* (p. 14).

Stenner, A. J., Burdick, H., Sanford, E. & Burdick, D. (2006). How accurate are Lexile text measures? *Journal of Applied Measurement*, 7(3), 307-322.

Vajjala, S. & Meurers, D. (2012). On improving the accuracy of readability classification using insights from second language acquisition. In *Proceedings of the 7th Workshop on the Innovative Use of NLP for Building Educational Applications*, 163-173.

Yngve, V.H. (1960). A model and an hypothesis for language structure. *Proceedings of the American Philosophical Society, 104*, 444-466.

Zeno, S. M., Ivens, S. H., Millard, R. T., Duvvuri, R. (1995). *The educator's word frequency guide.* Brewster, NY: Touchstone Applied Science Associates.

Author Index